Arab Strategies
and
Israel's Response

ABOUT THE AUTHOR

Yehoshafat Harkabi has had a versatile Israeli career: Company Commander in Israel's 1948 War of Independence, delegate of the subsequent armistice talks with Egypt, Secretary to Israel's Minister for Foreign Affairs (1949), Chief of Military Intelligence with the rank of Major General (1955–1959). He is a graduate of the Hebrew University (M.A. and Ph.D.) and Harvard University (Master in Public Administration). In 1959, he joined the Hebrew University, Jerusalem, as Professor of International Relations and Middle East Studies. As this book went to print in early February 1977, Professor Harkabi was appointed Advisor on Intelligence to the Prime Minister. He is the author of several previous works dealing with the Arab-Israeli conflict and strategic affairs.

Arab Strategies
and
Israel's Response

Yehoshafat Harkabi

THE FREE PRESS
A Division of Macmillan Publishing Co., Inc.
NEW YORK

Collier Macmillan Publishers
LONDON

Copyright © 1977 by The Free Press
A Division of Macmillan Publishing Co., Inc.

The Free Press
A Division of Macmillan Publishing Co., Inc.
866 Third Avenue, New York, N.Y. 10022

Collier Macmillan Canada, Ltd.

Library of Congress Catalog Card Number: 77–70273

Printed in the United States of America

printing number

1 2 3 4 5 6 7 8 9 10

Library of Congress Cataloging in Publication Data

Harkabi, Yehoshafat
  Arab strategies and Israel's response.

  Includes bibliographical references and index.
    1. Jewish-Arab relations--1949-   2. Israel
--Foreign opinion, Arab. 3. Arab countries--
Foreign opinion, Israeli. I. Title.
DS119.7.H3686   327.5694'017'4927   77-70273
ISBN 0-02-913760-8
ISBN 0-02-913780-2 pbk.

Contents

Preface   *ix*

Part I. The Arab Side   1
  Chapter 1. The Old Thinking: Arab Policies of
      the Fifties and Sixties   3
    From objective to program   3
    War *à outrance*—Nasser's version   8
    Guerrilla warfare   13
  Chapter 2. The New Thinking: Legacies of the
      Six-Day and Yom Kippur Wars   17
    Three schools of thought   17
    Incrementalism—from all-out war to
      limited wars   19
    From legitimacy of program to legitimization
      of objective   22
  Chapter 3. Arab Demands: Israel's Withdrawal
      and Solution of the Palestinian Problem   27

] v [

Contents

Chapter 4. Views of the Three Arab Schools
   of Thought   41
The "erosion and withering away" school   41
The "reducing Israel to its natural
   dimensions" school   47
The "continuous strife" school   63
Peculiarities of these schools and their
   constituencies   70

Part II. Israel's Policy   79
Chapter 5. A Personal Avowal   81
Chapter 6. The Evolution of Israeli Policy   85
Overview—Israel and the Arabs in the
   world's eyes   85
1949–1967   90
1967–1973   94
After 1973   100
Chapter 7. The Question of Concessions   111
The need for concessions   111
Objections   122
Conclusion   125
Chapter 8. Three Israeli Schools of Thought   127
The "dovish-dovish" school   128
The "hawkish-hawkish" school   133
The "hawkish-dovish" school   140

Chapter 9. The Arab and Israeli Schools of
   Thought Compared   153
Chapter 10. Conclusion   157

Notes   169

Index   191

Contents

List of Tables

Table 1. Old versus New Arab Thinking   23

Table 2. Schematic Typology of the Three
Arab Schools   74

Table 3. Differences between the Three
Israeli Schools   150

Preface

I arrived at the Center for Advanced Study in the Behavioral Sciences at Stanford in July 1975 hoping to take a leave from Middle Eastern dilemmas, and particularly from the strains of the Arab-Israeli conflict. I intended to devote my sabbatical year to compiling material for a philosophy of international relations. However, the Arab-Israeli problem haunted me relentlessly. Furthermore, as an extreme irony, the Arab-Israeli situation appeared instructive even within the framework of a philosophy on world order and symbolic of the perplexities of the collective human condition. The present essay is the product of recollecting the emotions of this conflict in the tranquillity of the Center. I am very grateful to the Center for enabling me to study and ruminate in solitude, while surrounded by the warmth of its friendly staff.

Since the completion of the manuscript a few
months ago, we have witnessed the petering out of
the Lebanese civil war by Syria establishing its control. The Lebanese upheaval reminded Arab rulers of
the precariousness of the internal order in some Arab
societies and admonished them of the radicalizing
effect of the Arab-Israeli conflict, thus creating a desire for some pause or respite in order to mend Arab
fences, recuperate and redress the havoc this war has
wrought in inter-Arab relations. This trend has caused
what I have called "the second Arab school of thought"
to become dominant in Arab councils. The weakening
of the PLO produced a concomitant diminution of the
main opposition to this school, as even the PLO now
struggles to adapt itself to this school's precepts.

Thus the possibility of a negotiated settlement looms
larger on the horizon than ever before. Still, what can
be stated with some confidence is not that peace will
be the outcome of such negotiations, but rather that
more people entertain such a hope, which in itself is of
political importance, though not decisively so.

Personally, listening to and reading what Arabs say
in their mass media, periodicals and books, watching
their internal polemics and public debates, I am not
convinced that their position has substantially mel-
lowed to the point of readiness to end the conflict and
accept Israel for good, even within its pre-1967 borders. True, Israel cannot expect that the Arabs would
recognize the legitimacy of its *establishment*, but Israel
is well justified in demanding their recognition of the

legitimacy of its *existence*, and its right to continue to exist, i.e., that the Arabs will give up once and for all their intention to see Israel's demise under whatever pretext or form. The excuse by Arab spokesmen that dreaming about such an end is permissible is dishonest. As the deliberations on how to implement such a dream are a major Arab national preoccupation and a main topic in Arab debates, it becomes an objective, a design and a program, and is not at all an "innocent" dream.

The Arab attitude is like an iceberg which consists of a tip representing the *political* or *diplomatic* position, as expressed in statements by leaders, and a massive body—the *national* position—consisting of ideological tenets, national philosophies and public discussions on the details of their stand. Any modification of the tip—the diplomatic position—in the form of moderate or "warmer" declarations of policy cannot really be effective if its underpinnings in the national position remain frozen solid. Change should start at the top but then its warmth should percolate downwards. In Egypt there are signs of change, of conflict weariness, and of fatigue with the Egyptian embroilment in the Palestinians' problem. However, in Syria the change is limited to tactical considerations and does not extend to the final objective of causing Israel's dismantlement, to which Syrian leaders continue to cling.

What has changed remarkably in Arab thinking is the modality by which Israel's demise is expected to be achieved. Previously, this objective was to be realized by an all-out war, whereas now an incremental process starting with Israeli contraction is prognosticated. The incremental process is more moderate because of its milder rhythm, even if it is meant to lead to the same end. Nevertheless, this moderation may have a feedback on the thinking about the objective which thus can be maintained with less urgency, less vehemence and greater forbearance. This change to a calmer process of slower and gentler motions may afford diplomacy an opportunity to produce a situation in which the Arabs, in order to get back most of the territories lost in 1967, would have to terminate the conflict and forgo any further pressures on Israel. Such a settlement should be solidified by concrete arrangements. To stress the Arabs' allegiance to their old objective to undo Israel is not to predict how they will behave; rather it serves as a reminder that this is what they are resolved to do if they are not prevented energetically from doing so. Thus the negotiations may assume the form of a tug-of-war between the attempt to freeze the situation and arrest the conflict in all its forms and Arab efforts to leave the door open to further exertions against Israel. Arabs tend to demand definite steps—withdrawal—from Israel and want to reserve open-endedness for themselves.

Some Arabs are mistaken in belittling the vitality of a smaller Israel. Provided peace does furnish Israel with reasonable assurances for its security, a period of revival may commence as Israel is freed from the

burdensome liability of governing the Arab popula-
tions in the occupied territories. Israel's adjustment to
the conditions of the peace settlement may become a
purgatory process relieving it of the sediments which
the conflict produced, thus causing a big transforma-
tion of its social, cultural and political life toward the
realization of the Zionist vision. Peace is still far away;
Israel's neighbors are still seething with hostility. Yet
this may subside, not by ignoring it in an autistic
ostrichlike fashion, but rather by facing it squarely,
counteracting it with a mixture of moderation in offering concessions and firmness in insisting on the termination of the conflict by word and deed.

The subject matter of this book is too sensitive politically to share or engage the least responsibility for
its ideas by even mentioning the few people who read
the manuscript and commented on it. I thanked them
privately. I would, however, like to express my grati-
tude to Mary Tye, who typed the manuscript with
great care, and to Miriam Gallaher, who skillfully
weeded out language oddities. Both are at the Center
for Advanced Study in the Behavioral Sciences. I
would also like to thank Charles E. Smith and Elly
Dickason at The Free Press, whom I have never met
but whose caring hands I have felt from afar.

I am indebted to Robert K. Merton whose assistance
was of inestimable value.

PART I

The Arab Side

one

The Old Thinking: Arab Policies of the Fifties and Sixties

From Objective to Program

A political plan consists of two major parts: the objective to be attained and the program—how the objective will be realized. These two components are dialectically related; the objective or objectives determine the program; the program, including the means it proposes to manipulate, imposes feasibility limitations on the objective.

A transition in emphasis characterizes the development of Arab thinking concerning the Arab-Israeli dispute. In the fifties, Arab discussions dealt chiefly with the objective, whereas at the present stage Arab thoughts gravitate more toward deliberations on the program.

In the fifties, the purpose was described as the liquidation of Israel as a polity, i.e., "politicide"—the destruction of a state. It was frequently expressed blatantly, with no verbal camouflage. The term most often used was *qada 'ala*—to put an end to. True, there were myriad other formulations, but they all meant the liquidation of Israel and some even alluded to the extermination of its people.[1] Israel existed owing to a concentration of Jews; its liquidation was predicated on putting an end to that concentration. No wonder that expressions of hatred and vilification for Jews as people who had created Israel and supported it were commonplace. Nevertheless, the objective of liquidation did not stem from simple malice; basically it reflected a philosophy that, on the one hand, liquidating Israel would right a wrong done to the Arabs because the country might then be restored to its Palestinian owners and become Arab, and, on the other, it would remove a foreign element disturbing the homogeneity of the area and threatening further incursion and expansion.

The Arabs did not simply hate Israel in a blind emotional way, but rather rejected the Israeli state in an ideological fashion, elaborating in great detail the reasons for their collective attitude. True, emotions and ideas or reasons are interconnected, and the negative attitude toward Israel on the cognitive level was reflected in hatred on the affective level. Nevertheless, an attitude on the cognitive level is probably more decisive. The affective level may influence immediate impulses, whereas the cognitive-ideological level is more important in the long run in molding political considerations and political behavior, so long as the ideology commands loyalty.

The Arab position toward Israel in the fifties was a consistent continuity of the Arab stand prior to 1948. During the British Mandate period (1917–1948) Arab efforts were mainly *preventive* in nature, aiming to forestall the establishment of a Jewish state. Once such a state was established, the aim became *restorative*—how to go back to the previous situation, or "normalcy," as President Nasser explained in a speech to the UN General Assembly in September 1960. However, restoration required the effacement of the unpleasant existent structure, the state of Israel. The Arab task became more difficult, since to prevent the establishment of a state is easier to justify and to accomplish than to undo it.

Arab thinking on the conflict struggled with two main issues: one moral-political—the *justification* of politicide; the other practical—the *feasibility* of such an objective. Most of the arguments justifying the liquidation of Israel were borrowed from those propounded during the Mandate period, for the reasons given why such a state should not be allowed to emerge were identical with those justifying its elimination. Convincing non-Arabs that Israel had to be destroyed, or that it had to be superseded by an Arab state, produced a problem for the Arabs, with which they had to grapple throughout the conflict. The problem was aggravated by the absolutist-totalistic nature of the politicidal objective, which was not susceptible to a partial satisfaction and compromise, as what was meant was the entire liquidation of Israel, not its truncation. One's self-confidence in one's objective can be impaired by failure to convince others of its legitimacy. Thus adherence to politicide as an objective was accompanied by uneasiness in articulating it. Expressions calling blatantly for the destruction of Israel gave way to euphemistic, indirect, eliding phrases: the objective became only "the liberation of Palestine," "the return of the Palestinians," or, in a later period, the establishment of a "democratic Palestinian state." Such phrases, though couched in positive, palatable terms, all presupposed the demise of Israel.[2]

Persuading themselves that the objective was feasible was a much more difficult task, particularly because of a theoretical awareness that world order has become somehow more rigid and inimical to boundary changes and that politicide is an anomalous political objective, as in the majority of historical conflicts the political entity of the rivals has been accepted and recognized and the conflict has been limited as a quarrel on a region between the contestants or on the order of superiority between them. There was too a practical consideration—apprehension that the international community, and in particular the West, might intervene and foil Arab efforts to destroy Israel. Such a foreboding apparently was much more worrisome most of the time than respect for Israeli strength, which because of the basic asymmetry between the

Arab world and Israel in human and physical resources Arabs tended to explain away as transient.

These two categories of arguments—one justifying the objective of politicide and the other asserting its feasibility—are dialectically interconnected. Belief in its justice could give rise to the expectation that eventually it would happen, as history would not indefinitely tolerate such an injustice, while a belief in its feasibility could reinforce the conviction in its justification.

Still, the rarity of politicide as a national objective in modern times, fear of intervention from the West and of Israel's strength, and consciousness of Arab weaknesses produced grave forebodings and gnawing doubts as to the practicability of the objective of destroying Israel. Thus the Arab position has been ambivalent, torn between faith in the prospect of realizing the objective, on the one hand, and skepticism of its feasibility and, for lack of a better alternative, acquiescence to the existence of Israel, on the other. However, the main thrust remained advocacy of liquidation.

The most trenchant argumentation for the feasibility of the objective would have been the presentation of a detailed program. However, the preoccupation with the objective in the fifties was attended by almost an absence of programmatic deliberations on how it would be attained. Perhaps the need for a program was not felt urgently and pressingly, as the dismantlement of Israel was not considered imminent. Thus the program was cavalierly disposed of by a slogan—or a figure of speech. Possibly the absence of serious discussion was due to apprehension that it might unfold difficulties in achieving the objective and erode confidence in its attainment. Paradoxically, in spite of the violent nature of the objective of destroying a state, its achievement was from time to time described in nonviolent terms. The Arabs would not be even required to go to war, because Israel would collapse under the weight of an Arab boycott and blockade, as if sheer Arab enmity were sufficient to decree Israel's doom. Liquidation, however, more often was expected to come in a military showdown, although its details and timing were not spelled out.

Another feature of the Arab stand in the fifties was that no particular role was assigned to the Palestinians in the struggle against Israel; they were simply shunted aside from the picture. This was due partially to their dispersion and weakness but more due to the reluctance of the Arab states to allow them to organize themselves. Furthermore, their main contribution was to be in implementing the program, which was not then the order of the day.

War à Outrance—*Nasser's Version*

With the passing of time, concentration on the objective seemed insufficient. The internal dynamics of the Arab position called for the elaboration of a program. President Nasser, with his stature as a leader and an ideologue, was spurred on to propound strategic thought and offer guidelines for a program. It would be an exaggeration to ascribe this trend to Nasser in person, but under his regime a spate of publications dealing with these subjects began to appear—more than in the past and most of them published in Egypt.

In the majority of Nasser's utterances on the Arab-Israeli conflict—as in many articles and books of his period—the objective was still to liquidate Israel by direct Arab action. Limited war was considered deficient as it could achieve only limited objectives. Thus the monumental task of obliterating a state called for an all-out war *à outrance*—to the bitter end—as the means of bringing it about. Liquidation was indivisible, since what was meant was liquidation of Israel in its entirety, not a partial liquidation that would leave a smaller Israel to exist. The indivisibility of the objective required indivisibility in the program, not a gradual unfolding of it—not its achievement in an incremental fashion, but rather its consummation by one event. Hence by logical consistency the act of surgery to undo a state called for the cataclysmic operation of an all-out war. The absolute nature of the politicidal objective called for an absolute means.[3]

A political objective can be achieved at one stroke by an *event*, or by an incremental, piecemeal, step-by-step, gradual *process*. The question of choosing between these two alternatives—liquidation by a spectacular event or by a process—loomed continuously in Arab thinking. *Prima facie* an incremental process is more practical. Nevertheless, President Nasser rejected the incremental approach in the two forms in which it appeared in the sixties. He rejected the *political* incremental approach advocated by President Habib Bourguiba of Tunisia. Bourguiba proposed in 1965 that the Arabs demand that Israel first implement UN resolutions, and specifically withdraw to the boundaries of the November 29, 1947 UN Partition Resolution.[4] Either this would weaken Israel, as preparation for a later stage to which Bourguiba alluded without spelling it out, or, if Israel refused to comply, the Arabs' manifestation of readiness for peace on the basis of the 1947 resolution would improve their stance in the international arena. Nasser rejected this proposal on the ground that a political settlement could lead to a compromise and was incompatible with the removal of Israel as a political entity. From time to time in the years 1959–1966, the Syrians proposed, though equivocally, an incremental *violent* process involving starting limited military action. Nasser rejected such a line, arguing that the Arabs should not indulge in prematurely engaging Israel in a limited war which could be escalated by Israel into a large-scale war and thus court defeat for the Arabs. Though the Arabs could absorb reverses, they should be aware of their possibly devastating internal effects. Nasser's prophetic premonition of such a situation foreshadowed the Six-Day War. Any war against Israel should be a final, decisive war and should only be undertaken if the Arabs could hope to gain ascendancy over Israel.

Such a war, moreover, would have to be brief, to

forestall intervention by the West. For that purpose the Arabs would first have to attain a position of crushing superiority, enabling them to topple Israel with lightning speed. That superiority, which is a function of military strength-building, Nasser explained, was predicated on internal reforms—political, economic, and social. There was a need, he stressed, for unity among the Arab states, so as to mobilize their collective potentialities and prevent wastage of energy in inter-Arab rivalries. It was necessary to achieve self-sufficiency and industrialization. Arab society would have to be transformed so as to bring about greater social cohesion and to make the individual soldier a better fighter. A revolutionary change in the social structure of all Arab states was a *sine qua non* for unity because unity demands homogeneity of regimes, "the unity of the objectives," as Nasser called it. Thus the road to war against Israel was lengthened, as intermediate internal targets of modernization of Arab societies and their merger had first to be achieved. President Nasser, it seems, believed that the Arab urge to prevail over Israel provided a strong motivational force that could be harnessed to drive the Arabs to embrace such social and political reforms, as well as that such reforms were a necessary condition for Arab victory in the eventual war.

Such preparations for war were bound to take a long time, and the struggle with Israel would therefore be protracted. It would be a contest encompassing many spheres—political, economic, social, and cultural—and culminating in an all-out war. Nasser's position was thus a blend of the extremism in the notion of all-out war and self-restraint in postponing it. Such a postponement signified an Israeli success in proving the unfeasibility of the Arab objective at least in the near future. Postponement could be a first step toward discarding the objective and the notion of war. Nasser emphasized not only that he had no plan which would be a shortcut to the goal but that such a shortcut was impossible, and he ridiculed the Syrians for cherishing the idea that war could be soon initiated. He continued to think that way, even though in 1967 he was driven into a series of actions that precipitated a war.

An intention expressed in an ideological or political attitude is real and serious the more the agent entertaining such an intention takes preparatory action to implement it. The Arabs deliberated extensively on the instrumentalities they would need to acquire in order to realize their intention, and justified them and the sacrifices they demanded precisely on the score that they would lead to the objective, even if they were also part of a general national program of modernization and nation building. Programmatic thinking spilled over to activities in many fields, such as economic warfare, boycotts, use of the oil weapon, closing the water passages of Suez and Tiran to Israeli traffic, political warfare to isolate Israel, political action within the Arab League, building military strength, military industries, collaboration between Arab states to set up a coalition, harassment over the borders and subversions, propaganda, prevention of Palestinian assimilation into Arab societies, pressure on Israel by use of Palestinian refugees, "spiritual mobilization" (indoctrination), etc.[5]

Guerrilla Warfare

The idea of a long drawn-out struggle implied that the Palestinians had to wait patiently. As a reaction and by way of seeking their own shortcut, active circles among the Palestinians developed a doctrine of *fedayeen* strategy of guerrilla warfare, which could start immediately without waiting for social and national reforms.[6] Rather, such a struggle would trigger social and national reforms by the heat it would generate and the example of its heroic feats. Furthermore, the people's participation in the struggle would drive the Arab public to overcome its passivity (*salbiyya*) and would thus be an all-powerful incentive for its mobilization. The guerrilla movement would spread and become a people's war. Such a war would not be a spectacular event à la Nasser, but a long process of attrition in which Israel would be bled to death and in which her technological superiority and any external intervention to save her would be to no avail. This program, which signified a turn to incrementalism in its violent form, drew inspiration from the successes of guerrilla warfare in China, Cuba, Algeria, and, after a time, Vietnam.[7]

Yet the relevance of such examples and the analogy

drawn from them as a warrant of success in the Arab-Israeli case was problematic. A necessary condition for effectiveness of guerrilla warfare is that it become an internal war, the uprising of an oppressed people against its rulers, or at least draw local popular support for the rebels. Mao Tse-tung has compared the propinquity of guerrilla fighters and the indigenous people to that of the fish and the water. The Palestinian ideologues of the *fedayeen* correctly observed that in this case the rebels (the Palestinians) were abroad, and that therefore their first task was to penetrate the country so that they could rise against the powers-that-be. But they overlooked the effect of this limitation on the prospects of waging guerrilla warfare against Israel. In Israel, inhabited by Jews who did not side with the guerrilla fighters, the Arab "fish" could not survive in the "water." The subsequent coming of the West Bank under Israel's control did not materially change this situation. Small wonder, then, that their concrete achievements in guerrilla combat were marginal, albeit some of their acts of terrorism could attract worldwide attention. It is doubtful whether guerrilla warfare suits as a matter of principle the conditions of the Arab or Palestinian objective. To repeat an explanation I propounded in a 1971 article called "The Weakness of the Fedayeen": "By means of guerrilla warfare France could be persuaded to give up Algeria, but no amount of guerrilla activities could bring the French to relinquish their sovereignty over France. A guerrilla warfare was instrumental in inducing the Americans to withdraw from Vietnam, but no guerrilla activities could press the Americans to leave the USA."[8]

The *fedayeen* movements came out vigorously against the policy followed by Ahmad Shukairy, whose principal objective was to establish a "Palestinian entity" to play up the Palestinian problem in the international arena and acquire political saliency for the Palestinians.[9] The *fedayeen* professed to aim at a tangible *military* result, the defeat of Israel. There is historical irony in the fact that their main achievement has been precisely the one they had spurned, *political* recognition and publicity. They renounced Shukairy and yet have become his heirs in terms of the end they have achieved. This, it should be stressed, came about as a result of the aid and support of the Arab states, whose importance on the world stage has grown so much of late, as well as the persistence of the Palestinians.

In the face of the Arab debacle in the Six-Day War, the concept of destroying Israel by conventional warfare lost credibility. The military defeat was too overwhelming to sustain the hope that Israel could be overcome on the battlefield in a clash between regular armies. Thus it gave a temporary boost to the *fedayeen,* and their organizations won considerable prestige in the Arab world, as the only active element which kept the banner of the anti-Israel struggle flying.

Before long, however, setbacks in that struggle exposed the *fedayeen* weakness. Since they had only a restricted presence in the territory under Israel's control, in which they had meant to carry on their guerrilla warfare, they became dependent on outside bases, such as Jordan. They competed for influence with the Jordanian authorities to the point where they began to menace the regime. Not only did they claim the loyalty of the Palestinian population in Jordan, and thus undermined its allegiance to the Jordanian throne, but also, in enjoying exterritoriality in Jordan and freedom from Jordanian control, they infringed upon Jordanian sovereignty and interfered with the functioning of the Jordanian administration. The old smoldering fundamental contradiction between the PLO and the Jordanians flared up in a showdown in the autumn of 1970, in which the *fedayeen* were defeated. It can be surmised that Jordan dared to rout them utterly because their failures in Israel had tarnished their prestige. After their expulsion from Jordan, their scope of activity was circumscribed even more narrowly to occasional incursions, mostly from the Lebanese border, and sporadic acts of terrorism in Israel and abroad.

two

The New Thinking: Legacies of the Six-Day and Yom Kippur Wars

Three Schools of Thought

The mortification of the Six-Day War sharpened the senses and refined the conceptions of Arab national debates. A period of reckoning and soul-searching began, of seeking answers to crucial questions: What was the secret of Arab weakness? Was the defeat due to accident or a basic flaw? How did circumstances now affect the possibility of Arab actions? How could they gain political backing which would make it possible for them to change the political situation and launch military initiatives?

The Six-Day War did not impress Arabs as a disproof of the feasibility of the Arab objective, though it strengthened doubts about it. At first, the conception of the *fedayeen* was allowed to dominate. But their military weaknesses were too salient to be explained away. Arab political thinking veered from the objective—its justification and the narrating of the history of the Arab-Israeli conflict, etc.—to more practical thinking and the elaboration of a program and a strategy of action. This change is reflected in the language used. Preoccupation with the objective and its justification called for the use of emotive language with great amounts of vituperation, reviling, invective, and abusive language. A comparative study of abusive language used by nations in conflict situations would be helpful in understanding conflicts and gauging attitudes. My personal guess is that in such a study the Arabs would be found to have used a great deal of such language.[1] Indeed, Arabs have frequently reproached themselves for resorting to invective in arguing against Israel, as deleterious to their cause. In the literature dealing with the programmatic issue, the semantic climate has changed and the frequency of invective has declined. The discussion flows in a much calmer tenor.

As propounded by the Arabs, the objective of destroying Israel commanded to a very great extent a consensus in their societies and showed homogeneity in conception. As their thinking moved to the consideration of the program, their conceptions became richer and more varied. Gradually three major conceptions emerged as three schools of thought embracing political and strategic thinking. The Arab arsenal of ideas and argumentation was elaborated in the big debate after 1970 on the attitude the Arabs should adopt toward Security Council Resolution 242.[2] The conceptions of the three schools were refined after the October 1973 War, and became three distinct idea-poles, even though not equal in intellectual quality or in terms of the support each has enjoyed. For the sake of convenience I shall call them:

The "erosion and withering away" school of thought

The "reducing Israel to its natural dimensions" school of thought

The "continuous strife" school of thought

Incrementalism—From All-Out War to Limited Wars

Before I analyze the elements of each of these conceptions and what distinguishes them, let us first consider what is common to them all. They all signify a return to the incremental-process approach, though their interpretation of it varies. Nasser's belief that a limited war would not be a viable possibility for the Arabs was disproved by the October 1973 War, even if in the military field its final results were far from successful. It proved that limited war can be an instrument to force Israel to withdraw and comply with further Arab demands.

The role of war has changed. Nasser considered war as a final act by which the Arabs would achieve their objective, and as the end to politics. By contrast, the present conceptions consider wars as interwoven into the political process, as wars of limited objectives like the October 1973 War. Of course, if a war of this kind is successful, its objectives may be expanded beyond the original intentions as a *coup de grâce* to Israel. But as some Arabs argue, Arab armies should not rush to cross over the pre-1967 lines, since that might give rise to international opposition. For the time being, maximum advantage should be derived from the fact that, internationally, Israel is regarded as a conquering power.

The new ideas influence the level of preparations needed in order to launch a war. For fighting a limited war which may not even end in an Arab victory, it is not necessary to have such superiority as would allow the Arabs to overwhelm Israel in one strike. Thus there is no longer a need for extravagant preparations and a long period of gestation.

The new ideas reflect a different attitude to the world's political environment. Nasser labored under two apprehensions: that Israel would escalate a war intended by the Arabs to be limited and that the West would intervene to save Israel. The new conception relies on such an intervention by the big powers to prevent escalation. The big powers will intervene to prevent any of the sides from achieving victory, yet such a policy is basically favorable to the Arabs. Limited war, which before was considered a risky step, became a favored one, and its goal changed to serving as a means of pressuring Israel to shrink. The same applies to *détente*, which Nasser regarded as adverse for the Arabs because it enabled the big powers to intervene. It has now become a means of mobilizing pressure from East and West to limit the hostilities and save the Arabs from a possible defeat.

In terms of military doctrine, the Arabs must prevent the ability of Israel, fighting on "inner lines," to concentrate its strength to win a decision on one front while containing the enemy on all other fronts—a strategy the Arabs call "separate treatment." In 1948, 1956, and 1967, Israel gained military advantages by exploiting this strategy. To avoid this, it is enough to have cooperation and coordination among the Arab armies to exercise pressure simultaneously on all fronts, and there is no need for a political merger.

The demands flowing from these conceptions are therefore much more moderate than the conditions stipulated by Nasser for launching war. The force of the inhibitory factors against war has somehow diminished.

The role of guerrilla warfare in the new conceptions has also changed. In the previous doctrine of all-out war, its function was marginal, hardly mentioned. In the *fedayeen* doctrines, guerrilla warfare had a central role. In the parlance of Fatah's ideologues, it was a "strategy, not tactics"—i.e., the main mode of combat. In the new conceptions, with the differences of emphasis, its role is more moderate—as tactics and a form of support, by guerrilla operations of harassment and attrition, mainly during the spells between wars.

The previous notion of culmination in an all-out war suffered from two major shortcomings: a practical one, the endless preparations needed for it and the difficulties in launching it; and a political one, the stigma it imposed on the Arab position as warmongering. Nevertheless, Nasser's view had the merit of internal consistency between the extremity of the objective (politicide) and the extremity of the means (all-out war). The new thinking succeeds in managing the inconsistency in its advocating an incremental process despite the absoluteness of the objective. However, such a change may impinge on the objective, which at most can be not the destruction of the state of Israel, but *making it unviable*, leaving subsequent developments to bring about its demise.

The difference between the old and the new thinking can be outlined in Table 1.

From Legitimacy of Program to Legitimization of Objective

The new Arab thinking frees the Arab position from heavy burdens. Preoccupation with the final objective and its difficulties gives way to a program of action composed of limited steps, in the form of demands addressed to Israel. Such demands may appear reasonable, calling for the rectification of limited grievances. Focusing world attention on these demands and isolating them from the situation that may transpire once they are met serves to evade specifying the obligations devolving on the Arabs against the fulfillment of their demands. Such a position has great merit in

TABLE 1: OLD VERSUS NEW ARAB THINKING

	Old	New
Objective	Destroying Israel	Mostly making Israel unviable
Modality of achieving the objective Incrementalism	An event, as an all-out war	A process
	Self-defeating, negating the indivisibility of the objective	Feasible, as limited war can be employed
War and diplomacy	War as end of politics; all-out war will achieve the final objective	Wars interwoven into the political process; war instrumental to pressure Israel
Preparations	Long and thorough; achieving superiority requires a total transformation of Arab society	Short; changes in Arab societies will be triggered by achievements in the struggle against Israel
Inter-Arab relationship	Unity is prerequisite for actualization of all potentialities	Minimal unity through collaboration is enough
The West	Is inimical as it will intervene to save Israel	May serve to keep war limited
Time dimension	Liquidating Israel is delayed until preparations consummated	Process of political pressures punctuated by threats and operations; no need for delay

the field of public relations, as it beclouds the absolutist-totalistic nature of the Arab position, i.e., its demand for full realization and its intolerance for compromise, giving it the semblance of relativism. Furthermore, it produces the impression of a moderate pragmatic Arab attitude liberated from the shackles of the traditional Arab politicidal ideology. However, pragmatism about a program does not necessarily imply moderation, and flexibility about tactics may still be coupled with rigidity about strategic goals. Incrementalism is not necessarily a moderate or conciliatory position, as its moderateness is limited to the means and not the ends, which may be harsh.

This evolution in the Arab position should not be treated in sordid, macabre terms as elaborating a position by guile against an inquisitive public opinion. International public opinion willingly went along with it, inasmuch as it freed people from the inconvenience of facing politicide as an objective in world politics. For the Arabs it is the outcome of a search by trial and error for a way to make their position more credible to themselves in terms of practicality, and more presentable to others. It provides a new solution to the old issues of "justification" and "feasibility."

The legitimacy acquired for the new programmatic thinking can serve almost unnoticeably as a means to confer legitimacy on the objective. Hence the stumbling block of justifying politicide can be overcome, or rather circumvented. Instead of being preoccupied with the final objective, articulating it for themselves and declaring it to others, and making politicide the center of gravity or pole around which the conflict revolves, the Arabs now make demands which they present to Israel as the crux and center of the conflict, as if a solution depended only on their fulfillment. Thus legitimization is achieved for the program by decoupling it from the final objective, or deferring to a later stage the unfolding of the connection between them.

: *three* :

Arab Demands: Israel's Withdrawal and Solution of the Palestinian Problem

The three schools of thought adhere to the two Arab political demands: (1) Israel's withdrawal from all Arab-occupied territories; (2) solution of the Palestinian problem—the restoration of the Palestinians' legitimate rights or the implementation of their national self-determination. Both these demands are cloaked in equivocation, which gives the three schools some leeway in their interpretation.

The ambiguity of the first demand stems from the possibility of understanding it to have a broader meaning than withdrawal from the areas occupied in 1967, as "the occupied territory" has in Arab political language been the conventional name for Israel in its pre-1967 boundaries.[1] Thus the gamut of meanings can range from the old politicidal objective dressed in an elegant formulation to withdrawal from the areas conquered in 1967, a more restrictive meaning. For those calling for the demise of Israel, such a formulation is seized upon as a useful verbal stratagem concealing its politicidal meaning, while for the more moderate, the broader meaning can produce some discomfort in public relations.

The demand for withdrawal is anchored in Security Council Resolution 242. The second demand is an addition whose meaning may be sinister. For once Israel withdraws to its pre-1967 boundaries, the place to establish the Palestinian state, as the means of solving the Palestinian problem, would be the West Bank and the Gaza strip, outside of Israel's boundaries. Thus the demand to set up such a state should logically be addressed to the Arab states of Jordan and Egypt, which during a long period of eighteen years from 1949 to 1967 could, if they had wished, have set up a Palestinian state. Unless this demand for solution of the Palestinian problem has hidden *geographical* meanings (i.e., that Israel should contract further and concede more land, or all its territory, to the Palestinians) it has, as far as Israel is concerned, only a *diplomatic* meaning—to waive opposition to a Palestinian state—or a *financial* meaning—to compensate the Palestinians for their lost properties in Israel. For the Arab states, the demand has a *concrete* meaning, which is to let such a state come into being. The fact that the demand is emphatically addressed to Israel and not to the Arab states gives rise to the suspicion that it does have a broader territorial meaning.

From the official documents and utterances of the

PLO one can learn that the solution of the Palestinian problem means superseding Israel by setting up "a Palestinian democratic state" over the *whole territory* of Palestine.[2] Mr. Farouk Kaddoumi, the head of the Political Department of the PLO and head of the PLO delegation to the January 1976 discussions at the Security Council on the Palestinian problem, in an interview with *Newsweek* summed up the Palestinian stand as follows:

> I am saying that the Israelis have two choices: to let all Palestinians return to their land and have this democratic state we propose, or to live in this so-called state of Israel without letting the Palestinians return. If they choose the latter, they will surely die and we will surely win.[3]

Mr. Kaddoumi serves an ultimatum. Either the Israelis allow the Palestinians to flood Israel (and thus presumably undermine it), or they will "die," presumably not a natural death. In both cases the results may be quite similar. If the Israelis insist on preserving their state and refuse to let it be liquidated, they themselves will have to be physically liquidated. Politicide is predicated on genocide, and the two are organically linked.

Sometimes Palestinian spokesmen expressed themselves in more moderate terms—by agreeing to a Palestinian state on the West Bank or "a state in the homeland"—followed by a denial by a more authoritative personality. One of the recent cases is that of Mr.

Ibrahim Sous, the PLO observer at UNESCO, who declared to *Le Monde* on December 25, 1975, that there could be a nonbelligerency treaty between a West Bank and Gaza Palestinian state and Israel. This was followed by an announcement by his chief, Mr. Kaddoumi, that "Sous was not authorized" to make such a statement and that "a lasting and durable peace can only be conceived in the establishment of a democratic state over the whole of Palestine." This announcement appeared in *Le Monde*, December 28, 1975. Mr. Sous corrected himself to the same effect in the same issue.

These games of hide and seek recur. They only testify to some uneasiness, in the face of public opinion, that some Palestinians feel concerning their real intention, which is the superseding of Israel by a single, or "unitary," Palestinian state. Thus honesty (a declaration of their intentions) and political expediency (the concealment of them in more savory terms) clash, producing verbal acrobatics and diplomatic writhings. Arabs frequently deny that they mean the destruction of the state of Israel in order to set up the Palestinian state on its ruins, claiming that if the Israelis peacefully submit and agree to shed the special personality of their state ("de-Zionize" it) by changing it from "Israel" to "Palestine," there will be no destruction. Thus responsibility for destruction is gracefully shifted to the Israelis. Yet it makes very little difference whether Israel is destroyed deliberately or only as a by-product of achieving a more sublime goal. Goals can always be arranged in a hierarchical order, aiming at higher values.

As the final proof of high morals, Palestinian spokesmen declare their readiness "to live with Jews," which, too, only means reluctance to coexist with their state, or simply politicide in disguise.

The PLO has consistently rejected the idea of a Palestinian state on the West Bank and Gaza strip as satisfying the Palestinians' national aspirations.[4] Probably the PLO does not think it could become a viable state, for, being landlocked, it would depend on Jordan and/or Israel for an outlet—which could give these states leverage over it. Furthermore, the establishment of such a state would place the Palestinians in two states—Jordan and the Palestinian state—which would be competing and possibly hostile. It would force the Palestinians in Jordan to make a choice hitherto evaded between being Palestinians and being Jordanians and by necessity identifying themselves with Jordan as the country they live in. Jordan would not permit about half its population to owe allegiance to a foreign state and would press for such a decision. No greater tragedy could befall the Palestinians. Therefore, the Palestinians' ambition is to have their state supersede Israel—and Jordan as well. There are, at the present, no signs whatsoever that the PLO would consent to accept a Palestinian state on the West Bank and Gaza as its share of a final settlement.

Self-determination for the Palestinians does not

mean merely having the right to develop their national personality. The Political Committee at the Tenth Popular Palestinian Congress made it very clear that self-determination is a euphemism for the destruction of Israel when it stated:

> The right of self-determination as regards the Palestinian people means [the right of] liberating the entire homeland and the establishment of the national Palestinian state. This is the scientific and legal meaning of the right of self-determination.[5]

According to this definition, recognition of self-determination for the Palestinians would amount to signing a blank check, giving the Palestinians the right to *determine* the character of the whole of Palestine, presumably on the basis that because they are called Palestinians, they are the lords of Palestine. The Palestinians claim for themselves what they deny to others.[6] There is, thus, an ideological imperative in the PLO position to consider the Israelis as not constituting a national unit deserving self-determination and a state.[7] The Israelis are a sub-human group which may have private rights as individuals but not any collective national rights.

The Palestinians are adept at coining catchwords. Tactics in propaganda and public relations have become an important component of the Arab programmatic thinking. When the politicidal meaning of their slogan "democratic state" became evident after Arafat's speech in the UN on November 13, 1974, they contrived a new formula to the effect that the democratic state constitutes only a "dream," a harmless vision, arguing that people in the depth of their misery should be allowed to find innocent consolation in indulging in daydreams. In justification, they presented a spurious symmetry—the Zionist dream and theirs. But if this be so, since Zionism is so harshly condemned, their "dream" cannot escape condemnation. Furthermore, their dream is not at all a naive catharsis, but a central programmatic tenet. Mr. Sous, in his correction in *Le Monde* of December 28, 1975 of his first statement specified: "It goes without saying that to achieve these objectives (the democratic state), the PLO foresees a multiform struggle, both political and military, against the Zionist state." Thus the slogan of the democratic state is an *antidream*, as a plan of war and the shedding of blood.[8]

As part of the program, it is argued, the Palestinians should derive full benefit from the UN resolutions which endorse their legitimate rights. Some advocate that they should invoke the Partition Resolution of November 1947 to induce Israel to evacuate territories which it has held since 1948–1949. Another resolution that Arabs cite is that of the General Assembly of December 11, 1948, whose Paragraph 11 stipulated (though with some reservations) that the refugees be permitted to return to their homes or else be given compensation. Compensation is, however, proscribed by Arab nationalism, and, according to Arab interpretation of the resolution, the Palestinians must demand the right to their landed properties.[9]

The demand to let all Palestinians return is couched in warm, homely terms of repatriation and of allowing them to return to their "homes," albeit these are by now nonexistent.[10] It equates all Palestinians with refugees, and refugees with people without homes and shelters. Both equations are factually inexact.

In 1947 there were 1,273,000 Palestinian Arabs. Their number, it is estimated, has now reached 2.9 million, including about 400,000 Israeli Arabs. About one-sixth of the Palestinians, i.e., a little less than half a million, live in refugee camps; the standard of living in these camps has improved and in the West Bank it is not significantly lower than that of the population surrounding them. "Refugee" is a legal category which is not necessarily economic, and many Palestinian "refugees" are well-to-do. About 75 percent of the Palestinians live within the territory of Mandatory Palestine before 1922, i.e., Israel and Jordan.

Arab spokesmen are discreet on the implications for Israelis of such a return of the Palestinians to their "homes," as it would require a mass eviction of Jews. Thus the return of the Palestinians is not only an explicit objective; it has practical *programmatic* significance as a means to undermine Israel by causing an internal catastrophe and a change in the balance of population.

The PLO position represents the absolutist-totalistic

nature of the Arab position in most blatant terms. It is depicted in the PLO basic document—the National Covenant—the endorsement of which is the main condition for admittance to the PLO. The rejection of Israel in it is unconditional as a matter of absolute principle and is implied repeatedly in almost half of its thirty-three articles. Such a rejection as the Covenant stipulates follows not only from a political position—which is volitional and can thus be changed—or an announcement of interests which is susceptible to partial fulfillment, but from a definitional tenet formulated as an axiom and an eternal truth that the Palestinians and Palestine are inseparable and that Palestine forms an indivisible unit and an integral part of the Arab patrimony (Articles 1 and 2). It affirms that the Palestinian Arab people should exercise their sovereignty over the entire area of Palestine and only thus can realize their self-determination. The liberation of Palestine (i.e., the elimination of Israel) is elevated as fateful for all the Arabs, as if "the destiny of the Arab nation, and indeed Arab existence itself, depend on the destiny of the Palestinian cause" (Article 14). Thus it is an existential imperative. It parades a host of utilitarian arguments concerning the good that will accrue to the Palestinians, the Arabs, and the world from the disappearance of Israel. The Palestinian and Arab struggle against Israel is a universal mission on behalf of sublime values. Documents such as the Mandate enacted by the League of Nations and the 1947 Partition Resolution of the UN are to be abrogated high-handedly. The PLO Covenant describes the Jews (significantly it does not refer to the Israelis; in fact, neither did Arafat in his speech to the UN when he spoke of the "Jewish man," meaning, of course, the Israelis) as undeserving of statehood, inasmuch as their only collective right is to be assimilated within other nationalities; they do not have the right to enjoy the uplift emanating from belonging to a collectivity. The Jewish attachment to the Holy Land is spurious, its centrality in Jewish culture is false.

Such a Palestinian position is extremely one-sided, self-centered, without any consideration for the adversary. It polarizes the conflict into absolute terms, good and evil. Only the Palestinians have rights. Their personality is described as "a genuine essential and inherent characteristic" (Article 4); it is eternal, it cannot lapse as a metaphysical entity. Only the Palestinians deserve self-determination, which means the right to all the country. They arrogate to themselves rights which they are unwilling to grant to the Israelis. Self-determination for the Palestinians becomes a right to determine that the Israelis should not have such a right. It is this lack of any sign of reciprocity that characterized the Covenant and the Palestinians' position —repeatedly asserted in all their National Councils. The flaw in this position is that it is a most gaudy *absolutist* position, whereas it behooves us as human beings to strive in world politics to propound *relativist* positions—which means "behavior in accordance with our own interests without forgetting that the opponent has interests as well; faith and devotion to our national ideals without ignoring that the rival, too, has ideals, tribulations and dreams; a sober evaluation of reality and of the opponent's status as well as our own."[11]

Thus a relativist position strives to reach a compromise, whereas in PLO parlance "compromise" is a bad, derogatory term. "The Political Program of the PLO," adopted in its Eleventh Council (January 1973), stipulated: "To militate against the compromising mentality and the plans it spawns which are either contrary to our people's cause of national liberation, or aim to liquidate this cause through 'proposed Palestinian entities' or through *a Palestinian state on part of the Palestinian national soil*. Also to oppose these plans through armed struggle and political struggle of the masses connected to it."[12]

The nature of the PLO is depicted in the position it took at its last National Council convened in Cairo in June 1974. Pressure by Arab states had been exercised on the PLO to moderate its position in order to make itself eligible for participation in a Geneva Conference. As a result the old position of rejecting a Palestinian state in the West Bank was modified by an acceptance of a "Palestinian Authority" there. This term apparently was chosen in order to evade calling it a state which may signify a more final arrangement.

The "Ten-point program" approved by the Council stipulated:

The PLO will struggle by every means, the foremost of which is armed struggle, to liberate Palestinian land and to establish the people's national, independent and fighting authority on every part of Palestinian land to be liberated. (Article 2.)

This acceptance is conditioned on the stipulation that the door would be left open for a continuation of struggle against Israel:

The PLO will struggle against any plan for the establishment of a Palestinian entity the price of which is recognition, conciliation, secure borders, renunciation of the national right, and our people's deprivation of their right to return and their right to determine their fate on the national soil. (Article 3).

The Palestinian national authority, after its establishment, will struggle for the unity of the confrontation states for the sake of completing the liberation of all Palestinian soil and as a step on the path of comprehensive Arab unity. (Article 8).

Israel is thus expected to withdraw from the West Bank and expose its population centers to attacks from bases a few miles away without any obligations on the part of the Palestinians. I consider such a position strange and extremely objectionable.

The importance of the Palestinian position transcends the confines of Palestine vis-à-vis Israel. It is of major significance in the assessment of the Arab states' position, since at the Rabat Summit conference in October 1974 all Arab states endorsed the position that the PLO was "the sole representative of the Palestinian people" and thus the one authorized to formulate Palestinian demands. The diplomatic importance of the Rabat Resolution lies in its exclusion of Jordan as a claimant to the West Bank. More important politically, it implied the Arab states' abetment of the extremists' PLO stance. President Sadat of Egypt reiterates frequently that there would be "no bargaining on the Palestinian rights," which could only mean underwriting them in their most extreme version.

Thus the second demand the Arabs present to the world community and to Israel, in its various verbal guises, leans toward the extreme meaning of setting up a Palestinian state over the whole of Palestine. Arab moderation is still very relative and remains within the framework of extremism. Inasmuch as there may be other interpretations of this demand, it is necessary to examine how each Arab school of thought views it.

four

Views of the Three Arab Schools of Thought

The "Erosion and Withering Away" School

This school of thought acknowledges that its goal is the demise of Israel, which will be achieved—and this is its novelty—not by arms but by domestic developments within Israeli society, causing its disintegration.[1] The Arabs' role would be mostly catalytic in bringing this process into being by outside pressure. Thus the Arabs can wash their hands of the destruction of a state. It would not be their fault, but simply the necessary outcome of the artificiality of Israel.

Israel, this school contends, has prospered because it has been the heroine of a success story. Israel, ceasing to grow, will shrivel. Its weakness is that success and growth are an existential imperative for it, without which it will cease to attract immigration, capital investment, and political support. Hence the first thing the Arabs must do is undermine this image of success. Coercing Israel to contract and return to its previous borders might achieve this. Forcing Israel to pull back, it is argued, is not an act of uncalled-for hostility, but of justice, since Israel's expansion constituted an aggression. Furthermore, Israel was created as a safe haven for Jews; therefore it must be demonstrated that Jews are safe everywhere but in Israel, that only there do Jews get killed. This would undermine the very foundations of the Zionist ideal. The bankruptcy of Zionism would lead to the bankruptcy of Israel. The instruments to be used in causing Israel to contract would be both political and military. Fullest political use is to be made of Security Council Resolution 242, which this school is ready to accept as a *tactical* step to force Israel to withdraw. However, insofar as Israel refuses to shrink, it must be pressured by war. Whenever the political process of withdrawal comes to a halt, threats of violence or open hostilities must be utilized to reactivate it. Such wars can be useful too as means to undermine public morale in Israel by causing casualties, to which its population is most sensitive.

A withdrawal by Israel to the 1967 borders would not be the end. After that the grievances of the Palestinians would be put forward, and it would be necessary to make sure they were able to continue fighting Israel to secure "their rights," even if it were not feasible for the Arab armies to join them. Thus guerrilla warfare has an auxiliary role in interwar periods to harass the Israelis, and a more autonomous mission after Israel's withdrawal.

This school of thought does not oppose interim agreements and political arrangements. In a realist or Machiavellian fashion it does not consider them as imposing standing obligations or constituting barriers to the continuation of the conflict and further pressures on Israel. Obligations incurred by the Arab states through such settlements should not be a source of worry. Given the complexities of the Arab-Israeli conflict, no settlement, even the most comprehensive, could eliminate all bones of contention; thus there will always be an issue that can subsequently be used to reopen the conflict. There is no danger that the conflict would be finalized. At most, the Arabs should eschew any arrangement that symbolizes or concretizes the termination of the conflict.

The Arabs, this school maintains, have failed to understand the need for flexibility in tactical maneuvering. In advocating such a line, Elias Murqus, a leftist writer living in Lataqia, Syria, explained that in the international arena states have to play the diplomatic game and sometimes temporarily assume arrangements which afterwards they will rescind. As historical examples he cites France's agreement to concede Alsace-Lorraine in 1871, which was abrogated with World War I, and Lenin's tactics in regard to Brest-Litovsk.[2] Thus the Arabs should cleverly expand their demands as they advance, or, rather, unfold the more extreme meaning of their basic demands, which for tactical reasons it is impolitic to brandish at the present stage.

This school supports the Palestinian vindications in their extreme version. The Palestinians should not excessively worry or harbor suspicions that the Arab states are only interested in recovering their territories and will afterwards turn their back on the Palestinians. The plurality of Arab states ensures that there always will be some Arab states that do not accede to the settlement, that will ensure that the conflict stays ablaze and apply pressure to this effect on those states which are party to the agreement. Any political settlement that would entail Israel's withdrawal is favorable, as it will weaken Israel and facilitate Palestinian and Arab action afterwards. The Arab states, according to this school, cannot abdicate their responsibility, as the Palestinian problem concerns all Arabs and is not only a parochial Palestinian issue. The Palestinians should not fear the setting up of a Palestinian state, even on only a part of Palestine, as they will not be left alone to face Israel; and their small state will be used as a springboard for further action against Israel, until it gives way and resigns itself to its fate and to the establishment of the Arab Palestinian democratic state.

Compelling Israel to dwindle through military and political processes will undermine the confidence of its population in the future of the state. Israel's going nuclear because of forebodings about its inability to maintain its posture in a conventional arms race, this school argues, cannot make any basic change, for a nuclear threat cannot stop or deter the process of nibbling. The threat of the superpowers to use their nuclear arsenal against any state threatening a non-nuclear state will neutralize any such use of a nuclear capability.

External pressure will cause internal political and social crises in which the "contradictions" and the odium inherent in the Zionist state will burst open. On top of this, a change in the population balance will be effected by repatriating the Palestinians and restoring their property to them. These two processes will cause the Jewish state and society to crumble, and Israel will *wither and fade away.*[3]

True, the US and world Jewry will struggle to prevent the eradication of Israel. But, in the process of its contraction, this school argues, when the appeal of Israel as a glorious human achievement wanes, they will resign themselves to the idea and, eventually, to its actuality. Once Israel's demise is considered inevitable by a growing number of people, the justification for its existence and support will be eroded on the moral level.

Historically the methodology advocated by this school of thought is a refined version of Habib Bourguiba's proposal in 1965 to achieve the Arab objective in a step-by-step political fashion, which he called the "phases method" (*Uslūb al-Marāhil*), advocating that Arabs give up the all-out-war idea and demand rather that Israel withdraw to the 1947 Partition Resolution boundaries and thus make UN resolutions a primary weapon against Israel. In those days Bourguiba's proposals were considered nationally sacrilegious; now they have become good nationalism.[4] If the present starting point is inferior from the Arab point of view, inasmuch as the withdrawal to the lines of 1967 has yet to be achieved, the momentum of the pressure on Israel is reinforced by the Palestinian demands, which in the meantime have acquired greater recognition, as well as by the concept of cyclical wars—and above all by the strengthening of the general Arab position in the world due to the use of the oil weapon.

Briefly, this school of thought manifests much greater sophistication than the old crude position calling for the destruction of Israel. This school adopted the notions of flexibility and gradualism which have become fashionable in modern strategic thinking. Its ideas probably fascinate Arab intellectuals. It does not criticize the Arabs' objective of politicide, but only their *modus operandi*. It is more moderate in its terms, maintaining that the demise of Israel will not come brusquely, by Arab violence, but graciously, through the anonymity of a historical process. This moderation stems from an optimistic belief that history is on the side of the Arabs. Arab victory and Israel's demise are both manifest destiny. Arabs erred, this school deplores, by abrogating excessive responsibility in carrying out the historical purpose, instead of adopting a more modest role as merely its agents.

The "Reducing Israel to Its Natural Dimensions" School

This school of thought is the most important one in terms of the support it enjoys from some Arab states, in particular Egypt.[5] It signifies the center of gravity in the Arab alignment. It is motivated by the conclusion that Israel cannot be destroyed in war, and openly advocates recourse to political process. Its advocates argue that the Arabs' adherence to the idea of liquidation has harmed the Arab case. Arabs had dallied with an idea that was beyond their ability to implement and could not be the order of the day.

The "natural dimensions" school reproaches Arab leaders for a vain proclivity to register their inimical attitude against Israel at the expense of achieving results: They looked for a cathartic relief by verbal extremism instead of advancing their cause in reality. By continually brandishing the liquidation objective or even by their insinuation of it, Arab leaders only estranged world public opinion and provided Israel with political and propaganda excuses, justifying its refusal to withdraw.

From these considerations of political expediency this school comes to a more basic reasoning. A political position has to be consonant with the realities and spirit of the age. The state of Israel, with its 3 million Jews, is a fact which the world would not tolerate having wiped off the map. International commitments to the existence of Israel and the present world order do not allow it, at least in the foreseeable future. States and circles friendly to the Arabs, including the Soviet Union, are against it. Let not the Arabs indulge in idle dreams that the Israelis would like to return to their countries of origin, as by now most of them have no such countries. The Arabs should be realists and resign themselves to Israel's existence, or rather accept that Israel will continue to exist. This school, therefore, declares its recognition of the state of Israel as a fact.[6]

This is the most moderate of the three schools in its basic stand; and though it considers war a part of the political process to force Israel to contract, it is less pugnacious and less eager to resort to cyclical wars. The turn of the tide against Egypt in the second part of the 1973 war and the danger of the collapse of the Egyptian forces are still alive to dissuade the Egyptian authorities from resorting to war, even if psychologic- ally there is a tendency to suppress such memories. Egyptian spokesmen have stressed that reconstructing the towns on the Suez Canal did not mean that Egypt has henceforth abandoned war. This school of thought is ready to rely on political pressures and it gives great importance to world public opinion, to the need to enlist its support of the Arab cause and isolate Israel in the international arena. Nevertheless, it adheres to the conventional Arab demands and is very emphatic in its insistence that all Arab-occupied lands, which it specifies as those occupied in 1967, should be returned to Arab states. Israel, however, in returning them, does not deserve to get any concessions from the Arabs, since Israel is only giving back what does not belong to it.

On the Palestinian problem, this school harbors some unease in defining the rights of the Palestinians. Indeed, it is somewhat inconvenient for its adherents to acknowledge that the restoration of those rights is simply a euphemism for the destruction of Israel. Therefore the school tries to steer clear of any definition, arguing that it is not for it to engage in such a definition. Defining the nature of Palestinian problems and their solution is the exclusive prerogative of the Palestinians as represented by the PLO. President Sadat has repeatedly demanded that the PLO set up a government in exile, apparently in the hope that setting it up would have a moderating effect on the Palestinian position. Such a demand might even represent a hesitant attempt on Egypt's part to leave the responsibility for the Palestinian problem in the hands of the Palestinians. He has criticized the PLO for adopting extreme positions which are impractical politically.

Official statements of this school often reiterate that there can be no bargaining over the Palestinian rights. This only implies that they must be realized in their most extreme version as propounded by the PLO. On the other hand, we also find among the adherents of this school a more limited approach, that of being satisfied with a Palestinian state on the West Bank and in the Gaza strip, at least at first.

The general tenor of this school is less doctrinaire

and more humane and pragmatic than that of the others. Its spokesmen may be ready to grant that the Israeli withdrawal and the restoration of the rights of the Palestinians are difficult concessions for Israel to make, because then it may turn into a state whose very existence becomes questionable. For this reason, the Arabs must be wary not even to hint that their intention is to bring about Israel's demise. Arab grievances must be presented as plausible demands. One must explain that consenting to coexist with Israel, albeit reduced in size, constitutes in itself an important concession on the part of the Arabs, an act of grace, inasmuch as Israel's creation by an act of colonialist spoliation warrants the demand for its liquidation. Furthermore, UN resolutions bear out the need to cut Israel down to its "natural" size. If Israel contends that by withdrawing it will lose strategic depth, and that therefore it needs defensible frontiers and strategic positions, one can propose that international guarantees be given. But the Arab states have no obligation toward Israel to indemnify it for its strategic shortcomings. It will have to learn how to live as a tiny state in the region.

This school shows a willingness to coexist with Israel in the 1949–1967 boundaries. Its circles recognize the damage that the Arab-Israeli conflict has caused to the Arabs and to Egypt in particular, and they desire to extricate themselves from the vortex of the conflict. Acquaintance with the internal problems and predicaments of Arab societies strengthens this wish. Fear of the radicalization effects in Arab societies caused by the conflict's continuous tensions prompts the moderate regimes to seek its temporary abatement.

Egypt's most famous writers, such as Nagīb Mahfūz, Tufīq al-Hakīm, and Louis 'Awad, seem most concerned about the social and cultural havoc the continuation of the conflict wreaks in Egypt. Commendably they value the quality of life over political prestige. They consider the conflict to be corrupting in its wasteful diversion of efforts and in the excuse it gives the rulers to curb freedom. Their worries are centered on Egyptian society and its future, and they are not excessively Arab-oriented. Their position is known more from criticisms leveled against them than from direct pronouncements.

According to the Syrian *Ath-Thaura* of January 14, 1976, Nagīb Mahfūz said in an interview with the Kuwaiti *Al-Qabs* on January 7, 1976: "I am interested in peace and agree to such a peace, even if it is conditioned by concessions on parts of territory. Territory itself is valueless. The goal is important and our goal must be the construction of civilization. We sacrifice man and send him to war to die for the goal. Why shall we not sacrifice territory if it is required for a goal which is more important than all other goals and which is peace for the sake of civilization?"

These courageous words are an exception. It is significant that he could speak thus. The circle of intellectuals holding such views is apparently small, and their *political* influence is minimal. Still, the fact that such a group exists is very important and should be hailed.[7]

One must not minimize the importance of the change which the second school signifies, as against the traditional Arab position, nor belittle the difficulties it had to overcome. The opposition in Arab ranks to the second school and its own apologetics to justify its stand only attest to the extremism of the traditional position. The difference is in both program and immediate objective, or, more precisely, in the feedback effects of difficulties in the implementation of the program upon its objective. Even qualified expressions of readiness by Arab political leaders to reach a settlement with Israel may have cumulative importance. Such declarations do not now sound blasphemous to Arab ears as they did in the past, and may gradually produce a public climate more congenial to settlement. True, the traditional position concerning the final objective has not vanished, because the political settlement the second school envisages is not a final, real, and positive peace with diplomatic and commercial relations, but a negative one—merely the absence of violence, or at most nonbelligerency. Thus, downgrading their significance, Egypt has stressed that interim agreements should be only military and not political. Granted, leaping from enmity to the intimacy of real peace relations would be improbable in the case of the Arab-Israeli conflict. Peace has to grow. But here there is explicit insistence that it will not grow, or that its growth be deferred; as Sadat has been saying, peace is far away—for the next generation to decide upon. Hence, in the meantime, the possibility of switching from this conception to the first one, of "erosion and withering away," stays open, and the lack of concrete content to this kind of peace may facilitate the shift.

The first and second schools of thought have much in common in ways and means, the difference being mainly in evaluating the final situation that will emerge when their shared demands are realized and in their prescriptions for Arab action at that stage. Whereas the first estimates that in such a state of affairs Israel will no longer be viable and *deliberately* seeks to bring this about by maintaining pressure until Israel is dismembered, the second takes into account the possibility that a small Israel will somehow survive. It holds that there is no absolute certainty either way, and is vague, discreet, and noncommittal on the question of what the Arabs will do then.

The main feature in the second conception is that it is deliberately *open-ended*. While it jettisons the liquidation idea, it elegantly retains an option of reverting to it in the future. It stresses that the political settlement it has in mind is not a peace which entails the final termination of the conflict. What is more, its adherence to the idea of stages may imply that beyond the stage of having Israel withdraw loom further stages of contraction and pressure until Israel is eliminated, especially if the circumstances are propitious.[8] Thus open-endedness is not merely an attribute but apparently a programmatic central strategic doctrine.

Spokesmen of this school often express themselves in such a way that one may doubt if there is any real significance to the difference between this school and the first one, or wonder whether the second is merely a dressing of the first school in more presentable diplomatic attire. Expressions by spokesmen of the second school which give rise to such a suspicion abound. Khālid Mūhi ad-Dīn, a member of Nasser's original group in 1952 and Chairman of the Egyptian Council for Peace and Justice, and presently the leader of the "Left Platform" within the Socialist Arab Union, the only political organization allowed in Egypt, has written: "This is my view, which I have expressed on every occasion. The Security Council Resolution and all UN Resolutions are a means which in the international domain will enable us to enlist public opinion in our cause. We are of the opinion that there is an urgent campaign to defeat the present aggression. Unless we defeat it, we shall be unable to defeat the earlier one; if we cannot defeat the 1967 aggression, we shall by no means be able to defeat the 1948 aggression. This is a conception which we do not attempt to conceal at any Arab meeting, international or local. The obligations of the Arab states do not bind the Palestinian revolution. We do not think that the realization of the Security Council Resolution, if it is destined to be realized, will be to terminate our struggle with Israel."[9] "Defeating the 1948 aggression" means undoing the establishment of the state of Israel.

Spokesmen of the second school, notably Egyptians,

sometimes explain that Egypt's agreement to coexist with a smaller Israel is only a political stratagem and that carrying out Resolution 242 is only an essential step toward the achievement of the "national goals" ("national," in Arabic *qaumi,* means in this context transcending the more limited objectives of Egypt for the sake of the wider ones of Arab nationalism). They tend to eschew spelling out what these "national," or pan-Arab goals are, as if they are generally known and tacitly understood by all the Arabs. Hence satisfaction of its demands would not deflect Egypt from its commitment to Arab national aspirations. These two sets of goals are frequently differentiated in the spokesmen's parlance as short-range and long-range strategy and tactics, or the responsibility of this generation or the next one. Sadat stated in an interview in *Al-Anwār* of June 22, 1975: "The effort of our generation is to return to 1967 borders. Afterward the next generation will carry the responsibility." Sadat has repeated the same theme in other speeches and press interviews. No one can speak for or commit future generations. Stressing this as Sadat does may imply that one's own obligations are only of a provisional nature. Sadat reiterates, too, that he does not discuss in public final objectives or strategy. For instance, when discussing his attitude toward settlement, he said: "I do not want to place my cards before the microphones" (as quoted by Cairo Radio on September 8, 1975, in an account of the Sadat interview for the Kuwaiti *As-Siāsah*). Thus behind his readiness to recognize Israel, and to reach a settlement there are other designs which he is reluctant to discuss. It is difficult to escape from the impression that what Egypt seems to want to achieve is a combination of diplomatic flexibility and tenacity in adherence to the old Arab national aims in the conflict.

A commentator of the Egyptian radio station Voice of the Arabs (Saut al-'Arab) declared on May 24, 1974: "We have sacrificed a lot of blood and property for the short-range objective incorporated in Security Council Resolution 242, which all Arab States have accepted and whose execution they have demanded. Yet when we succeed in restoring lands and rights, while taking into account the dimensions of the international circumstances and our achievements, we believe that Egypt will reach the objective which it accepted as its responsibility toward the Arab world." Thus the execution of the Arab national objective is only postponed.

In a press interview, the Egyptian Ambassador in Kuwait was asked: "Is the meaning of those Resolutions [242 and 338] that the Arab States have given up Palestine to Israel?[10] Why does the Summit Conference [Rabat] speak about the boundaries of 1967 and not about Palestine in its entirety?" He replied: "The wise man sets phases to reach his objectives. The serious man who relies on deeds and not on words presents his words phase after phase. The present circumstances on the Arab and international planes enable [us] to succeed only as far as [relates to] the objectives

which were announced in the Summit Conference"
(*Middle East News Agency* from Damascus, May 21,
1975). Here again the long-range objectives of regain-
ing all of Palestine is not discarded but only postponed,
as an expediency of the hour.

Hisham Sharabi, Professor of International Relations at Georgetown University, Washington, D.C.,
and editor of the *Journal of Palestinian Studies,* can be
relied upon when he asserts, "Those defending this
position [political settlement according to Resolution
242] stress that in their effort to achieve a peaceful
settlement they do not give up the goal of liberation,
but only 'postpone' it to a more appropriate time."[11]

Another tendency among proponents of the second
school is to downgrade Arab divergencies, whereas the
other two schools stress them as of utmost ideological
significance. According to Sadat, "There is no dispute
among the Arabs on destiny and the battle" (interview
on Kuwaiti Television, according to Cairo Radio, May
14, 1975). The divergencies are described as if they
had to do with marginal tactical issues. But does this
mean that on fundamentals, including "the long-range
objective," the so-called moderates see eye to eye with
the extremists?

An interesting case is Muhammad Sid-Ahmad, a
political commentator of *Al-Ahram,* in his 1975 book
After the Guns Fall Silent[12] and his reply to criticism
in *Al-Hawādeth* of June 13, 1975. Sid-Ahmad deduces
the need for peace in the Middle East from global
trends in world politics, and especially *détente,* which

must spill over to secondary conflicts. He stresses that
Israel should be integrated in the region and that it has
an important contribution to make toward the region's
development, as the convergence of "Israel's quality
with Arab quantity" will bear beneficial results. Yet, he
concludes that Israel will refuse to diffuse or submerge
its special personality in the region, and thus the conflict will continue. He recommends a change in the
PLO policy—namely, that it should demand the restoration of the 1947 partition boundaries. He supports
the "dream" of the democratic unitary state which he
sees as in the process of materializing. Furthermore,
he stresses that his plan constitutes only a change in
method and not in the basic Arab aims. Thus,
strangely, he combines a strong urge for peace with a
ruling out of peaceful coexistence. He excludes the
possibility of peaceful collaboration between the Arabs
and an Israel retaining its national character. Israel
should shed its special character by dissolving itself
(*tadhvib*) in its Arab environment and become Arab.

Luftī-al Khūlī scathingly criticized Sid-Ahmad, Dr.
Gamal al-Oteifi (Vice President of the Egyptian parliament), and Boutros Ghali (Editor of the Egyptian
"Al-Siassa al-Dawlya," a Yearbook of International
Politics) for the views they expressed in an interview
with Arnaud de Borchgrave in *Newsweek*, August 18,
1975, implying acceptance of some coexistence with
Israel. In rejoinders in the September 1975 issue of
the Egyptian *At-Tali'a* they explained their views,
which all maintained do not mean real coexistence

with Israel. Sid-Ahmad accused Borchgrave of distortions in reviewing his book in an earlier issue of *Newsweek:*

> He based himself on true selected references in order to attribute to me meanings which are not in my book and which, moreover, flagrantly diverge from its contents and text.[13]

Sid-Ahmad explained what kind of settlement he envisaged:

> What is said in the dialogue gives comprehensive settlement a definite meaning. It is not cancellation of the conflict and not a demand to give up final Arab goals—i.e. the wiping out of the traces of 1967 aggression and the setting up of the democratic secular state in all the territory of Palestine—but the continuation of the struggle by other methods, which are not aggression such as Israel has actually practiced in the last quarter of a century.[14]

Sid-Ahmad goes on to say:

> What are these other methods? They are those which actualize mutual benefit instead of causing mutual damage. This is the essence of what I wrote in my book. In order that this appeal acquires the force of credibility with "the others" in general, and with the "West" in particular, I do not say that our goal in settlement is the wiping out of Israel. I said: "Each side after the settle-

ment will prove that it is more capable in achieving its final goal without resort to aggression. . . . Nevertheless, I should stress that personally I never uttered in the dialogue even once the idea of "peaceful coexistence" as the basis of the future relationship between the Arabs and Israel even after the achievement of a general settlement, and I used instead the idea of mutual satisfaction in living together in the region. The term that I used —modus vivendi—is totally clear in this context.[15]

There is a baffling ambivalence in Sid-Ahmad's views. He manifests a willingness to relinquish the violent phase of the conflict and recognizes that henceforth changes in it will be accomplished by peaceful means. However, in his views there is no recognition of coexistence between the contestants, which implies leaving to each side to choose their internal regimes and ideologies. Israeli Zionism is proscribed. Moreover, Israel's existence is only temporary as he endorses the establishment of the Palestinian democratic state to supersede it.

Views similar to Sid-Ahmad's have appeared in articles in the Egyptian quarterly *Al-Siassa al-Dawliya*. These articles postulate coexistence between Israel and Arab states, even though only as a transient phase, winding up in a description of Israel's losing its uniqueness (or in their parlance, being de-Zionized) and melting away ("tadhvib"—dissolving, the verb they

frequently use) in its Arab environment. The Israeli
Jews will exist as a cultural religious community but
not as a nation. The unsavory association of such ideas
with the old Islamic attitudes toward the Jews as the
"Dhimmis" (the Christian and Jewish minorities living
on sufferance in a Muslim country where many restric-
tions were imposed on them according to Muslim common law) can hardly escape notice, even if there is no
evidence that the authors of these articles were in-
spired by Islam. (The editor B. Ghali, mentioned
earlier, is a Copt). Rejoicing that at least some Arabs
recognize real peaceful coexistence with Israel is
marred by the ephemeral nature of such a coexistence,
and the miracle becomes a mirage. Thus the demise
of Israel re-emerges, this time not in the form of a
harsh political objective but as a learned evaluation of
an inescapable historical process. Is this an elegant res-
cuing or salvaging operation of the politicidal notion,
or, as the Arabs do not serve an active role in the process, only a sign of reluctance to give up the idea of the
demise of Israel? That may be so, but as one considers
a trend which he favors as ordained, he may be
tempted to help history accomplish it. Personally, I
prefer to consider these views as sincere, without attributing to them ulterior motives, but I cannot be
completely relieved of doubts. Nationalism may eventually spend itself and the political structures of hu-
manity may change. However, to apply such a fu-
turistic pattern only to the Israelis and to reserve to

the Arabs the right to be in the throes of a most extreme nationalism does not manifest excessive idealism.

Pronouncements by Egyptian spokesmen to the effect that the difference between the second school and the other two are only tactical can be interpreted in either of two ways:

1. They are apologetic, addressed to Arab public opinion, including the extremists, to justify Egypt's opting for a political solution and its abandoning the objective of seeing Israel disappear, and are thus devoid of political significance as indicators of Egypt's real intentions. Egypt cannot quit its old positions offhand; therefore it registers commitment to them, yet voids them of political importance by deferring them to a far future. Its open-endedness is a subterfuge, used as an insurance policy against Arab extremists.

2. They reflect real intentions which Egypt does not divulge externally and which will be reinforced once Israel weakens its posture by withdrawals. Egypt will then exploit the new situation to transform its open-ended position into binding national objectives. Deferring the realization of an objective does not necessarily impair its meaningfulness. Nasser, whose commitment to the destruction of Israel was beyond question, also saw it as a long-range proposition. Its open-endedness is a strategic principle as regards Israel and a tactical stratagem as regards world public opinion. The conciliatory stance is only a means of pursuing the struggle.

Furthermore, one can argue that even if there is a significant difference between the first and the second schools and even if the present leaders of Egypt have genuinely given up politicide, still the internal dynamics of the Arab position will eventually drive the present leaders or their successors to the views and practices of the first school, and the Palestinians and extreme Arab states will put all their weight into pressing for these views and practices, once Israel abides by Arab demands and weakens itself. As Muhammad Hassanein Heikal (former editor-in-chief of *Al-Ahram*) once said, the Arabs cannot make war without Egypt, and Egypt cannot conclude peace without the Arabs.

I prefer to leave as moot the question of which of the above two interpretations is correct. Perhaps at present there is no answer to such a question, as future political circumstances will determine whether the second school sticks to its position or goes over and adopts the policies of the first and third schools. One may hope that the first interpretation proves correct, yet take precautions against the possibility of the second—or if possible, initiate action to prevent its materializing.

The "Continuous Strife" School

The third school accepts the idea of gradual erosion or incrementalism as expressed by the two previous schools, with one important reservation—that such a process does not necessitate or entail any interim political settlement, even transient.[16] The struggle against Israel should continue uninterruptedly, using all paraphernalia of violent and political means. Yet the exclusion of the political instrumentalities of a settlement tilts the balance into giving a greater role to violent means. Continuity of the struggle, which is the central operative idea of this school, impels it to put emphasis on guerrilla warfare as a continuum between wars and a support weapon during war. A truce or a pause in the struggle, adherents of this school say, is of great danger to the Arabs, in both its external and its internal aspects.

Externally, it may cause a permanent freeze. Israel will not agree to a political solution calling for its withdrawal to 1967 boundaries unless it is assured that the way to more Arab demands and further armed conflict is blocked. Israel will not retreat and enfeeble itself if the Arabs hold on to their option of taking up the armed struggle again and the conflict is not finalized. The international community will justify such a position on the part of Israel politically and, as far as the United States is concerned, practically in direct aid.

This school is adamant in its rejection of any political settlement of Resolution 242, and of participation at a Geneva conference, and is hostile to all US efforts to intermediate. The US wish to achieve a political solution and a compromise proves in the eyes of this school that it is inimical to Arab aspirations in the conflict.

Let not the Arabs indulge in the illusion, it reproaches the other schools of thought, that they will be able to unleash the conflict once there is a settlement, whatever its kind. The dishonesty of such a position will prove self-defeating. Intoxication with their own clever tactics to achieve it is bound to ensnare the Arabs in positions from which they will not be able to loosen themselves. Once a political settlement is reached, it may deadlock continuous Arab efforts. Thus an Arab effort to liquidate Israel in an incremental fashion punctuated by interim settlements might be deflected to become an incremental liquidation of the conflict. Incrementalism is acceptable only if it means a continuous pressure on Israel, culminating in its liquidation. Making Israel unviable is not enough, as assistance may still keep it alive. The Arabs have to give it a final *coup de grâce*.

Internally, an interim settlement or a pause might weaken the Arabs' resolve and curb their momentum. It would enable the diversion of their societies' attention to other pressing internal requirements. It might foster in the Arab public the false idea that there could be possibility of coexistence with Israel, which, combined with remembrance of the sufferings the conflict caused Arab societies, might impel them to abandon further action. The flame of the conflict should stay ablaze, as once it starts flickering it may go out.

The conflict, in the eyes of this school, is not at all a disaster; it has positive functions as a vehicle through which the modernization and revitalization of Arab societies might be achieved. It has, too, the merit of being an incentive to unity. Thus Arabs should not be impatient to rid themselves of it and be ready to pay for it in concessions, but rather should benefit from the galvanization of their societies it affords.

"War Is the Solution to Healing Arab Society from Its Ailings" is the title of an article in the February 2, 1975, issue of the Syrian armed forces journal *Jaish ash-Sha'ab* (The People's Army), in which the armed struggle against Israel is described as the most important front for all the Arabs and as "a front in which victory will lead to concrete and immediate victories on the fronts of disunity [of the Arab world] and backwardness."

Thus, whereas Nasser considered internal reform to be a prerequisite for the preparedness that would enable the launching of war and the second school considers the conflict as inhibiting reforms, in the third school's conception reform will come as a by-product of the struggle and of war.

Basically, this school represents the traditional Arab attitude against Israel, including the use of the old rationale that the conflict between the Arabs and Israel is a total one in which no compromise is possible, no matter whether Israel is truncated or becomes "a nonaggressive state." The eradication of Israel is presented as a historical inevitability. So long as Israel exists, the Arabs will suffer from an alienation by inability to develop their collective personality, actualize their potentialities, and modernize their societies. Furthermore, under any settlement the Arabs will pay a heavy price, for in according legitimacy to a reduced Israel they will as a matter of principle give up their denial of its right to exist and negate the Palestinians' claim to the country in its entirety. Any recognition of Israel, be it only *de facto*, means a *de jure* abandonment of nonrecognition. The famous "nays" of the Khartum Arab summit conference—no peace, no recognition, and no negotiations—epitomize this school's stand and are invoked by its spokesmen.[17] The conflict with Israel is nonstop, not a series of periodic clashes and wars. Moreover, the time factor is important and the Arabs should hasten. Israel's going nuclear may paralyze the Arabs' continuous activities against Israel even on the lower rungs of violence for fear of escalation. Changes in the international constellation and in the Arab world (reduction in the effectiveness of the oil weapon and the emergence of crises in Arab societies) may intervene as time passes by and impede the continuation of the struggle.

This school basically rejects the idea of the setting up of a Palestinian state on the West Bank as the solution of the Palestinian problem—even as a first step and a springboard to further advances. It sees such a project as fraught with the danger of becoming the graveyard for Palestinian aspirations. The new state would be caught between Israel and Jordan and squeezed by both of them.

The tactics of a temporary political settlement—so goes the pleading of this school as against the first and second—might block the strategic objective of politicide. There must be continuity between tactics and strategy. If the strategic objective is the elimination of Israel, it is self-contradictory to use tactics based on accepting its existence, even temporarily. Such tactics are not a sly ruse, as some Arab spokesmen have pretended, but a trap. Flexibility in tactics is commendable as long as it does not cause deviation from the strategic objectives. Strategy and tactics must logically be compatible in character and modality, and complementary to each other. However, by agreeing to the existence of Israel temporarily, as a tactical position and as an intermediary station on the path to its demise, which is the strategic goal, a dissonance is produced. It implies the subordination of strategy to tactics, a relationship which Arab radicals denigrate as "the tyranny of tactics" (*taughiān at-taktik*). Strategy must dominate tactics, not the other way around.

Among the extreme leftist circles belonging to this school of thought a political arrangement is derogatively considered a "reformist" step and a betrayal of the revolutionary vocation. Between the Arabs and Israel there is an "antagonist contradiction" in which any respite or settlement, even if transient, is intolerable. The revolution and the struggle should go on irrespective of obstacles.

This school tends to downgrade diplomacy as a means in the hands of the Arabs against Israel. It feels that diplomacy and the objective of politicide are incongruent (Nasser's basic stand). On the other hand, paradoxically, it upgrades the ability of diplomacy to impose fetters on Arab freedom to reopen the conflict after a settlement. This school tends to be cynical about the importance of world public relations and the need to enlist world public opinion to support the Arab side. It is vain, it maintains, to win over Western public opinion to support the Arab side, since eventually the politicidal objective will estrange it from the Arabs. The anti-Western bias of this school produces an inclination toward the East, and in particular, the Soviet Union; its protagonists feel that even if the USSR does not subscribe to Israel's demise, it may treat it with indifference.

The third school is pessimistic about leaving historical spontaneity to serve the Arab cause, as the first school advocates; the conflict is necessarily a continuous uphill battle. Its spokesmen call for Arab activism and are suspicious that the new idea of relying on the disintegration of Israel as the means of bringing about its demise is only a sign that the Arabs are abdicating their national responsibility of fighting against Israel, and showing an attitude of resignation to its existence. Furthermore, ironically, though the third school is most extreme in its anti-Israeli stand, it believes in Israel's capability to endure contraction, and not only to survive but to expand again.

From an Israeli point of view the third school inadvertently bears witness that there is a possibility of coexistence, and that the Arabs might be satisfied with less than the demise of Israel. This is exactly what this school directs its thrust against; its frenzied argumentations against such an eventuality only imply that it regards it as feasible, and that the *open-endedness* of the second school can be blocked.

Peculiarities of these Schools and their Constituencies

The three schools of thought have not been institutionalized to the same extent in demarcated self-conscious political collectivities. The first school is *ideological,* while the other two are *political* and are adhered to by Arab political actors and expressed in their political behavior in both word and deed. The terms I use to name them here do not exist as such, but are neologisms, though derived from phrases and catchwords used in Arab political debate. Their taxonomy is the result of an interpretive effort to present ideal types. In the real world there are mixed cases and, as is common in political life, views fluctuate and groups and individuals thus change their affiliations back and forth. The three schools also do not enclose in their fold all individual Arabs, since for many the conflict is not the subject of their daily worries and thinking.

In analyzing these schools of thought I have tried to organize their conceptions and thoughts into three systems or syndromes of ideas, so that each system is reasonably *cohesive* in terms of its internal consistency, as one idea logically leads to another in the system, and is reasonably *autonomous* in terms of its ideological distinctiveness. Nevertheless, these systems share some features. They all are occupied with the elaboration of a program of action as their main concern and do not excessively deal with the objective. Inevitably such programs of action relate to the objectives they seek to achieve; otherwise they would have no sense. For both the first and third schools the objective is that Israel as an independent Jewish state will cease to exist. Thus the two are closely related, their bone of contention being the worth of the political process, which the third school minimizes. The second school prefers to leave the objective issue pending, recognizing a feedback effect from the program of action, i.e., the influence of the modality of implementation on the objective. The objective is thus not articulated, because of either strategical or tactical considerations, affording two possible approaches within this school which give it its peculiar flexibility. Its insistent emphasis on the fulfillment of the Arab demands compensates for the ambiguity on the objective. The open-ended nature of the second school may eventually bring it closer to the first school. It is a possibility to reckon with. The most pronounced difference is between the second and third schools, which too could be narrowed down if the second should slide over to the first. Thus proximity and divergence between these three schools have an interplay.

In different degrees the three schools show uneasiness, not so much about the idea of politicide itself as about brandishing it or avowing that politicide is the net outcome of their more elegant formulations of the objectives or about proclaiming that their programs (or demands) lead to it. The first school in addressing a foreign audience hides its harsh objective by the lenience of the process and shifts the onus of blame to historical determinism. The second school finds refuge in agnostic innocence. Even the more outspoken third school hides the objective it set out to accomplish in positive terms of meting out justice, and it shows, too, a reluctance to spell out its politicidal implications.

No doubt the thinking in all these schools is of incomparably higher quality than previous Arab thinking on the conflict. The schools have succeeded in overcoming the difficulty in which the previous thought was enmeshed by breaking the bond between politicide and the strategy of all-out war, with the practical difficulties and the stigma such a program entailed. They all opt for incrementalism of one sort or another: the first school for incrementalism that leads inevitably to Israel's disintegration, the second for incrementalism expiring in an equivocal situation, and the third for incrementalism requiring continuous efforts.

One can discern in the new thinking a sense of controlled satisfaction in the Arabs' achievement, yet not a triumphant buoyancy. Many misgivings and doubts still linger, despite the urge to believe that because of their material superiority they will ultimately prevail.[18] After all, the success in formulating these programs has been mostly theoretical; the road to their actualization is still a lengthy one running through the vicissitudes of inter-Arab tension, the hazards of upheavals in the Arabs' societies, and vacillation in the international arena. For the third school such forebodings serve as a main point of departure.

The "erosion and withering away" school seems to represent a basic ideological conception, as the other two schools borrow from its arsenal of ideas, especially on the method of the gradual erosion. The paradox is that, although central, this conception is not the official conception of any Arab government. Nor has it been enshrined in any official document. It may be described as being on the Arab *metapolitical* level, which is to say that it is comprised within general ideological ideas and is at the bases of policies. Nevertheless, allusions to this school's ideas may be found in many statements of Arab politicians. It occupies a middle ground between the other two schools. It goes too far for the second school, and not far enough for the third.

Currently the "reducing Israel to its natural dimensions" school is politically the most important one among some Arab states—first and foremost Egypt. This conception recurs time after time in the words of Sadat. As has been noted, it does not imply a wholesale dismissal of the first conception; there can be a combination of the two.[19] Jordan, too, belongs to the second school, with an important reservation as to the need for an independent Palestinian state. Instead, Jordan has proposed an autonomous Palestinian region in a Hashemite federation. Apparently the second

TABLE 2: SCHEMATIC TYPOLOGY OF THE THREE ARAB SCHOOLS

	Erosion and Withering Away	Reducing Israel to Its Natural Dimensions	Continuous Strife
The objective	Disintegration of Israel, incremental self-liquidation	Contracting Israel, which may make its existence precarious	Liquidating Israel, to be superseded by the Palestinian state
Time	Disintegration is a long process, yet within foreseeable future	Peace and/or the demise of Israel is for the next generation	Liquidating Israel is not too long a process if the Arabs operate properly by hastening it
Means	Military and political	Mainly political; military too	Mainly violent
Role of regular war and guerrilla warfare	Regular war and guerrilla war as means of harassment and as auxiliary	War and threat of war to push the political process; guerrilla warfare marginal	Continuous guerrilla warfare, punctuated by regular wars
Meaning of demanding Israel's withdrawal	Extensive; is meant as a stage to weaken Israel	Restrictive; refers to all Arab territories occupied in 1967	Extensive; meaning will unfold with withdrawal
Meaning of the demand to solve the Palestinian problem	Extensive; a step in the process of causing disintegration	Restrictive; a Palestinian state on the West Bank should satisfy the Palestinians as a first step	Extensive; Palestine and Israel exclude each other
Attitude toward SC Res. 242	Its acceptance is tactical	Its acceptance is at the present stage strategic	Its rejection is fundamental strategy
Palestinians' role	Secondary, though they embody the main political grievance	Marginal, though they embody a main political grievance; should be attenuated	Central, but not exclusive; they ensure continuity of the conflict

	Erosion and Withering Away	Reducing Israel to Its Natural Dimensions	Continuous Strife
Main danger to Arab policy	Misunderstanding the historical trend	Irrealism, ignoring world order	Freeze by an interim political settlement
Ideological versus pragmatic motivations	Liquidation of Israel is both an ideological doctrine and a historical imperative; policy is subservient to ideology	Attention to diplomatic exigencies; dominance of political considerations over ideology; pragmatic	Ideological orthodoxy; inconsistency between ideology and praxis is self-defeating; pragmatism is bad realism
Stand toward West and East	West is basically an enemy, but may help in preventing the escalation of war	US support should be elicited to exercise political pressure on Israel; may limit war	West is mainly enemy; its commitment to Israel is deep and cannot be diverted; pro-Soviet
Conflict's impact on Arab societies	Less attention to this problem; apparently neutral, as both harmful and beneficial	Harmful; diverts resources and energies from internal constructive tasks	Mostly beneficial, producing strong motivation for modernization and revival, and an urge for unity
Approach to history	History favors the Arabs; optimism due to historical determinism	Arabs will succeed if they are realistic and understand the historical trends	Arabs will win if they understand the intrinsic value of the struggle and exert themselves
Israel going nuclear	Almost irrelevant as nuclear deterrence cannot stop nibbling	Arabs should go nuclear too	May paralyze Arab struggle on all levels
Locus, constituencies	Metapolitical level; holds attraction for intellectuals; influential as source of ideas; not institutionalized in any establishment	Moderate Arab states and some Palestinians, especially in West Bank, Communist parties	Extreme Arab states, PLO, and in particular the "Rejection Front"

school also has followers among the Palestinians on the West Bank. The Arab Communist parties mostly belong to this school, with the proviso that resorting to political means does not imply using the good offices of the US, but rather a "Geneva conference."

The "continuous strife" conception of the third school is most advocated in those Arab states called extremist—Iraq, Libya, Algeria—and in many of the Syrian pronouncements and among the *fedayeen* and the PLO. It is epitomized in the resolutions of the Palestinian National Councils. Its most typical expression is manifest today in the circles of the so-called Rejection Front because, in deference to such Arab states as Egypt, the attitudes of Fatah and the PLO establishment betray an ambivalence, a wavering, and a tendency to resign themselves to elements of the second conception, apparently in the hope that what will really happen will conform to the prognosis of the first conception, or even better to that of the third.[20] In their condemnation of the September 1975 Sinai interim agreement, the PLO and the Rejection Front have been very close. The need for a continuous and unrelenting struggle is stressed repeatedly in the PLO monthly *Shu'un Filastiniyya*.

Syria is a mixed case. Its leaders are aware of their dependence on Egyptian support for waging war, despite their hectic effort to build a basis of strength in the Eastern front countries. Furthermore, pragmatic considerations impel Syria to align itself with the *tactics* of the second school. This leaning is counterbalanced by direct pressure from the PLO and indirectly by the need to compete with Iraq as to which of the two represents the true version of the Ba'ath ideology, to which both owe allegiance.[21] Thus far Syrian leadership has adroitly managed the inconsistency of combining the tactics of the first and second schools with the strategy of the third.[22]

Table 2 is designed to summarize the main differences among the three schools of thought and their peculiarities.

PART II

Israel's Policy

: *five* :

A Personal Avowal

The analytical descriptive function of evaluating the behavior of foreign nations, or of an opponent, and the normative prescriptive function of policy planning should be inherently and institutionally separated. Evaluation of the situation under study serves planning by generating data for it. However, human frailty may distort this hierarchical relationship by making evaluation of the situation subservient to planning; thus people unknowingly may describe or assess the situation not as it is, but so that it tallies with, or rather supports, their policy recommendations. Such a proclivity has been both common and harmful. (This problem is extremely complex. Isolating the two functions may result in bareness. The solution lies in a

combination of separation and interaction, consciousness of the pitfalls and an effort to control them.)

I would have preferred to leave my description and
analysis of the Arabs' thinking on their program as it
stands and not delve into policy recommendations for
Israel. However, my description of the Arab position
may have, for the reader, a *suggestive* meaning as to
the policy Israel should have, which he may impute to
me as being implied by my description. Furthermore,
the reader's policy conclusions may have a feedback
effect in coloring his understanding of the descriptive
part. Thus, paradoxically, in order that my description
be understood properly, I must present my policy conclusions, even if the descriptive and prescriptive parts
do not necessarily constitute one organic whole, since
from the same set of data about the adversary, different policies can be deduced. Passing from descriptive data to policy prescription goes through the mediation of causality assumptions, i.e., assumptions that
certain deeds are conducive to desired outcomes. Such
assumptions may be presented as wisdom culled from
past experience and thus as following from the descriptive part, yet without having the same validity as the
descriptive data.

Hence I claim greater validity for the first, analyti-
cal-descriptive part of this work than for this second,
prescriptive one. The first stands on more solid ground
as an interpretation or rendition of the past and present, and its method is explicative, whereas the second

is more speculative, a venture on how to influence the present for the sake of outcomes in the future.

The fatefulness of the issue of policy for Israel in this difficult hour weighs on me very heavily. True, suggesting policy in an essay is not the same as making policy. Still, the feeling of responsibility overwhelms me. Where shall we find guidance? All the strands of the tragic Jewish history seem to converge on us, evoking the lessons which different generations and factions have learned from their ordeals and tribulations. But are they relevant? What is at stake transcends Israel's future, as it is momentous for Jewish destiny. Thus the Jews everywhere have both the right and the duty to offer their views on these issues and to participate in this grand debate.

I am haunted by questions of how I can be sure that the line I suggest stands a chance of success. Is it not too risky? The only warrant I can humbly furnish for the policy I advocate is personal belief in it, which does not carry much weight, and the cogency of my argumentation, which can be challenged.

six

The Evolution of
Israeli Policy

To arrive at prescription will require some survey of the development of Israeli attitudes, an analysis of Israel's dilemmas and the challenges the Arabs have addressed to Israel and Israel's responses. It will not be a narrative of events, but rather a sparse outline of an intellectual history of the conflict. Its terms will be general, steering away from polemics by not specifying names of persons and groups. However, anyone with a little knowledge of the Israeli scene will identify them easily.

Overview—Israel and the Arabs
in the World's Eyes

The challenge that the new Arab programmatic thinking poses for Israel is much graver than that of previ-

ous Arab stands. In order to understand the new problems facing Israel, we have to survey them against the
background of the older ones, and compare Israel's
previous behavior and needs with the present ones.
The Arabs, as mentioned earlier, have grappled with
the two issues of the *justification* and the *feasibility* of
politicide regarding Israel. In a general abstract fashion, Israel's policy throughout the conflict can be sum-
marized as counteractive; it has tried to prove by deed
and word that politicide is both unjustifiable and un-
feasible. The two thrusts of this effort were dialectically connected, as success or failure in one affected
the other.

Counteracting the feasibility nexus could be direct
and tangible. Israel had to build up its military
strength in order to deter all-out war as the means by
which Arabs hoped to achieve their purpose, and it
had to demonstrate that strength.[1] Israel was successful in proving unfeasibility, at least for the short term.
More effective was its demonstration that the political
objective could not be achieved by all-out war.

The task of persuading the Arabs that their objective
was unjustifiable was much more complex. By nature
this issue is flimsier and less tangible. In a conflict
situation it cannot be settled by open debate of any
sort. A rebuttal from Israel could hardly persuade the
Arabs, as their stand was fortified by their ideology
and their version of the history of the conflict. Some
thought that perhaps by showing greater understanding and empathy for Arab grievances, Israel could

make some limited impact.[2] However, recurring crises hardened the positions of the rivals and muted their responsiveness.

Deeds are another avenue of symbolic discourse. Perhaps Israel's being more forthright in offering concessions could have been such a political and symbolic act. However, Israel was caught here in a grave dilemma, for offering significant concessions from its narrow base of existence could have weakened its ability to withstand Arab pressures. It would perhaps have nibbled away at the justification nexus but at the same time strengthened the feasibility one. This malignant feature has attended the conflict, limiting Israeli freedom for benevolent action. As I wrote in 1965, "Israel, by the nature of her position, will prefer to exist dangerously to offering concessions that incur the danger of nonexistence."[3] Reluctance to offer concessions confirmed in the Arabs' eyes the negative image of Israel and strengthened their conviction as to the justification of their case. Israel's success in demonstrating its ability to undermine the feasibility of its destruction in turn posed a threat to the Arabs, which they tended to interpret as one that could only be cured in a radical fashion, by elimination of the source of the threat—and by this interpretation reinforcing the "justification" of their original objective. This dilemma, with which Israel has had to wrestle all along, symbolizes a major and perennial predicament of the human condition.

Israel's other avenue for influencing the Arab stand was indirect and vicarious, via the mediation of world public opinion. One can make a good case for the weakness of such an influence; still it has its merits, and the Arabs have been sensitive to criticisms leveled against them from the outside. Their consciousness of backwardness and weakness, of not occupying in the world the place they tend to think they deserve, the asymmetry between their numbers and physical resources on the one hand and their stature on the other —these may have augmented such sensitivity. The difficulties the Arabs have had in justifying politicide to foreign audiences, their unease at expressing it openly, and their need to find refuge in ambiguous, indirect, euphemistic expressions have all attested to such a sensitivity. National objectives cannot be esoteric incantations, for in order to mobilize public support they have to be brandished most conspicuously. Embarrassment over the politicidal objective externally may spill over internally, as the effort to separate these two domains cannot be completely successful. Making the opponent uneasy and apologetic about his objective is a first small step in the process of its *erosion,* inducing him to start discarding it. True, the indivisibility of the Arabs' traditional objective in the conflict and the absolutist nature of their position hamper its gradual change, as this would have to be accomplished in one big jump, by one qualitative change in principle. Still, Arab writings in its formulations have signified some change, if not always in context at least in the vehemence with which it is held.

In the Arab-Israeli conflict there have been a few

short spells of direct interaction, in negotiations between the rivals or in military showdowns. The rest has
been a lengthy competition in pleading one's case with
other states and to the public, so as to gain sympathy
and support. Big countries have political assets by
which they can affect reality directly, whereas small
states lack such assets and frequently can only use
public relations as a means of persuading the powerful
major political actors to affect reality in their favor.
The power of small states is thus in many cases vicarious and borrowed more than they are ready to acknowledge. This aspect is conspicuous in their need
for weaponry, the acquisition of which from the big
powers is dependent on the suppliers' good will. Impressing public opinion in the Western world is like-
wise a means to reach the decision makers in those
countries, who are responsive to some extent to opinions in their communities. Public opinion is fickle and
volatile, sometimes resigning itself to the accomplished
fact, thus endorsing it. At other times it influences
which facts will be accomplished.

Almost all through history the international system
was merely an arena for the interaction of the political
actors, without the system having political substance
of its own. Thus nations did not worry about the influence of the international system on the outcome of conflicts and did not consider the international system as
a factor to reckon with in their policy making.

The main development in international relations has
been some *reification* of the international system, its

acquiring systemic qualities which influence the inter-
actions between actors and their outcomes. It evolved
from being a neutral framework to playing the role of
a magnetic field, impeding or helping movement in
one direction or the other. This system is influenced by
public opinion and the stand of governments, especially when some kind of consensus emerges. Thus
public opinion may in some measure embody the spirit
of the age and represent the historical trend.

The importance for Israel of winning the support of
world public opinion is due in the first place to the
influence of world opinion on current political developments. Second, it may exert influence on the Arab
position, particularly on the core element of the Arab
position toward Israel—the politicidal objective. In order to win the support of public opinion one has to
present a good case for oneself and persuade others
that one's position is reasonable, while castigating the
rival's position as aggressive and unreasonable.

1949–1967

In the fifties, Israel did not have grave problems with
public opinion. It was a *status quo* power, and the territorial settlements of the 1949 armistice agreements
had more or less gained legitimacy in the eyes of governments and their publics. The Arabs wanted to
change the *status quo* and the onus of proof lay with
them—a situation aggravated by their politicidal objective. The brunt of public opinion was directed more

against them than against Israel; concerning Israel the issues were minor, such as the demand to let in groups of Palestinian refugees. This trend reached a climax a short time before the Six-Day War, when the Arabs' harsh and shrill politicidal declarations led public opinion to justify Israel's breaking the peace and launching a surprise attack.

From the beginning Israel should have seized upon the weaknesses in the politicidal position of the Arabs and harped on them, in order to mobilize the support of world opinion against such a position. As just as the Arab case might be, it could not justify politicide. Israel should have exploited the ugly features in the Arabs' position—the very high frequency of invective, vilification, anti-Semitism—so as to exert pressure on them; it should have demonstrated the organic connection between politicide, genocide, and the revilement of the Israelis and Jews. Politicide as a political objective produced a tendency on the part of many Arabs to describe Israel as fundamentally and deeply depraved, as deserving a death verdict, and from such a stand to consider its builders—the Jews and their culture—as evil.[4]

Strange as it may seem, Israel was slack and squeamish, as though wishing not to embarrass the Arabs and offend public opinion. Its spokesmen frequently played down the politicidal objective, refraining from describing it in all its ideological ramifications. They did not present it in *depth* as the tip of the iceberg of a well-elaborated ideological structure. On the contrary, Israelis supported the view that the Arabs were carried away by their own exuberance, as if they were victims of their rich and beautiful language which impelled them to say what they did not really mean, as if their words in Arabic did not reflect actual intentions. Thus politicide was explained away as a gambit in an oriental bazaar of overstating the price in order to settle for a moderate compromise. Such exegeses of Arab behavior are both false and morally repellent, as they imply contempt toward the Arabs.

True, Israel's leaders and diplomats protested that the Arabs desired to destroy Israel. But in face of Israel's proven strength such complaints could not be persuasive. They gave the impression either of dishonesty—a pretext for capitalizing on some Arab slips of tongue—or, more charitably, of being a fixation, a hangover from the trauma of the holocaust.

The anomaly of politicide as an objective produced an inclination in many foreign circles not to take it at its face value. Only the presentation of the Arab position in its ideological depth stood a chance of producing in public opinion a revulsion from the Arabs' politicidal position and its condemnation. Such a presentation could have elicited support for Israel's stand and an appreciation of its anxieties, dilemmas, and demands.

In a later period, mainly after 1967, Arab ideological positions were presented in Israeli official propaganda publications, but, as far as I remember, never in diplomatic notes or in political pronouncements by the chief Israeli leaders. True, it is not as effective to complain that one's rival indulges in an unpleasant ideology as it is to decry his wrong acts. Still, there would have been great worth not only in protesting the public hangings of twelve Jews in a central square in Baghdad in 1969 but in drawing the attention of public opinion, much earlier, to the great amount of anti-Semitic literature published under official Arab auspices, which may have paved the way for such hangings. The Israelis tended to fight back at the Arabs politically while the Arabs fought both ideologically and politically. Thus an imbalance was produced, which became more acute after 1967 as the Arabs used the Israeli occupation of Arab areas as an argument to castigate Israel, while playing down what caused this occupation.

The Israeli Parliament, the Knesset, never dealt with the basic issues of the conflict or the Arab position. The failing was general. The conflict and the Arab position were not a subject for research and instruction in Israeli universities, and only after 1967 did they begin to attract the interest of academics. Many of Israel's public leaders and diplomats were not acquainted with Arab thinking on the conflict, so no wonder they could not use such knowledge in Israel's diplomacy, or in their interviews and pronouncements.

A major obstacle in understanding the Arab position has been an inability by many Israelis to study it in isolation from its implications for Israel. Thus features in the Arab position which seemed discomforting have been discarded or ignored. The existence or nonexistence of such features has been ascertained according to the criteria good or bad, instead of true or false. Israelis have not been conscious enough of the possibility of distorting factors hidden in themselves affecting their judgment of Arab attitudes and of the need to try to overcome them by a healthy dose of self-criticism or some attempt at self-transcendence. The epistemological aspects of the conflict have hardly attracted interest. Thus all along its history the conflict has been ascribed to some misunderstanding between the parties which for the Israelis meant that the Arabs "did not understand." Semantically this can be established by the frequency of cliché found in editorials in Israeli newspapers and speeches of leaders didactically sermonizing: "The Arabs must understand, etc."

Perhaps a defense mechanism was in operation in Israel, inhibiting thinking about the conflict and its dangers for Israel. The internal efforts of building a nation and a culture diverted attention to other channels of energy.

1967–1973

The Six-Day War and the fact that world opinion blamed the Arabs for it taught the Arabs a valuable lesson on the need to pay attention to public opinion as an important factor. A grand debate opened on how Arabs should present their case in moderate terms. It was discussed at public, governmental, and intergovernmental levels, and recommendations were formulated, such as never to say "the destruction of Israel," but to say "the abolition of the Zionist entity."

On the Israeli side the effect of the war was completely different, almost the reverse. Although foreign public opinion was favorable, foreign governments' actions were a disappointment, as Israel was let down and left to fight alone. American assurances from February 11, 1952 on that the straits of Tiran were considered an international water passage and would thus stay open were proved of no worth when Nasser closed them. The deep anxiety on the eve of the war in face of the Arabs' sordid threats could not be erased by the victory. The Israeli public awoke to the realities of Arab hostility. Thus the Israelis demanded significant changes in the boundaries to improve Israel's strategic posture, so that the trauma of May 1967 would not recur. It was a slow process which gained momentum as it became clear that the conflict would continue on. Occupying these areas, with their old familiar biblical names, resurrected historical memories and gave rise to a feeling of attachment and reluctance to part with them. Yet at the basis of Israel's territorial demands lay first and foremost the search for security. For many Israelis, apparently, acknowledgment of this was worrisome in itself; thus they tended to give such territorial demands a Zionist and religious guise. The Zionist and religious motivation is indeed powerful; still, it is secondary to the search for security and is derived from it. It is significant that during 1949–1967 the Israeli public had resigned itself to the armistice lines, accepting them as permanent and allowing the Zionist and religious claims to hibernate to the point of apathy. The war and its exalting heroic feats seemed to many Israelis a justification for the territorial demands as a shield against Arab provocations in the future.

But Israel has been enmeshed in an ambivalence. Although the only justification for the demands for strategic territorial changes were the basically hostile Arab attitudes toward Israel, the legacy from the previous period of refraining from presenting them in their full significance and ideological depth continued—even when the need for such a presentation became more acute. Israel was entrapped in a severe contradiction. While its behavior and its territorial demands were motivated by the consciousness of Arab threats, its diplomacy played them down, if not always deliberately, at least by the colorless and anemic fashion in which it presented the Arab stand. The fault was general. Self-admiration for the victories perhaps also had the psychological effect of making the Israeli public believe there must be among the Arabs a greater resignation to the existence of Israel. Many Israeli leaders repeatedly pronounced in the period 1967–1973 optimistic prognostications about the prospects of peace, which they now try to forget. In Israel "pessimism" is a traditionally derogatory term. Thus genuine or ostentatious optimism has tilted the general view toward a rosy nonreality.

Describing the harshness of the conflict and the depth of the Arab opposition was frowned upon in many Israeli circles as gloomy paranoia, whereas soothing over the severity of the conflict and giving the Arab viewpoints heavy touches of makeup were a sign of mature judgment, broad-mindedness, and forbearance. One can suspect a vague belief in the magic of the self-fulfilling prophecy—that a harsh description of the conflict might aggravate it, whereas a moderate portrayal of the Arab viewpoints would exercise a moderating influence on them.[5]

Good tidings spread from the thesis that peace would flourish from good relations between Jews and West Bank Arabs, or would be ushered in through open bridges to Jordan. Such a gradualist incremental approach had an appeal for both Israelis and foreigners, despite the irrelevancy at the political level of friendly relations at the individual level and the lack of continuity from open bridges to political settlement. From the beginning it was clear that the West Bank Arabs were not an autonomous political factor that could conclude political agreements without the consent of the Arab states, particularly Jordan and the PLO. West Bank Palestinians reiterated that a political agreement must start with the Arab governments and the PLO, though eventually they would like to have their say in such a settlement. However, Israelis continued propounding theories about the possibility of the growth of a moderate leadership on the West Bank, and fancifully attributed to it the ability to reach an agreement. But moderateness was not the issue. Being moderate is probably a necessary condition for wishing a settlement, but it is not a sufficient condition for putting one in a position to conclude an agreement. Although West Bankers may be paragons of moderateness, this does not make them an autonomous political factor. It is not their failing, but the result of circumstances—their connections with and dependence on the other Palestinians and Arabs.

As a line of retreat, a learned theory was propounded that the West Bank Arabs could be Israeli partners in "micro" politics, i.e., in local government arrangements for utilities, public works, schooling, health, and so on; and this was true. However, real politics are *macro* by nature. No doubt Israel's liberal policy in the occupied areas was a great achievement in itself. Expecting it to yield a political settlement, and more so an agreement to an Israeli military presence on the mountains or in the Jordan Valley, amounted to overtaxing it to the point of absurdity. Indulging in the illusion of a political settlement with the West Bank Arabs had deleterious effects in that it spared Israel from the need to come to grips with the real Palestinian problem—the PLO.

Paradoxically, both moderate and extremist Israelis clung to the idea that the Arab position had become more conciliatory. The extremists needed this idea to substantiate their claim that Israel could hold on to the 1967 conquests and that the Arabs had already begun resigning themselves to their losses. The moderates needed it to support their claim that dovish gestures or initiatives from Israel would bring dovish responses from the Arabs, of which they already discerned moderate currents. Thus moderates and extremists, the government and the opposition, collaborated in playing down Arab motivation and belittled the efforts the Arabs were ready to make and the risks they were ready to take in order to change the results of the war by a new war.

Israeli policy oscillated, stumbling on its ambivalences. Consciousness of the Arab threat impelled territorial demands. Ogling for peace prompted downgrading the vehemence of Arab rejection. Israeli leadership, political and cultural, was inept in managing Israel's existential contradictions. This lack of coherence played into the Arabs' hands in their attempts to pose as moderate and to present Israel as intransigent, expansionist, covetous, egotistic, and callous to the sufferings and grievances of others. The Arabs maneuvered themselves into the position of plaintiff, and Israel was reduced to the role of defendant. In world public opinion the Arabs won a victory, ironically with the aid and collaboration of the Israelis, who erred both by omission—failing to present the extremeness of Arab positions—and by commission—pointing to Arab moderateness.

These placid attitudes spilled over and influenced the internal social climate in Israel. Holding the strategic areas occupied in the 1967 war gave Israelis a sense of security. Dangers receded, the weakness of

the Arabs was proved, peace—or at least Arab resignation and acquiescence to coexistence—was prophesied.
All of this contributed to a false sense that the collective goals had been achieved and thus everyone could
preoccupy himself with improving his personal lot.
The rot had set in. It was this placidity that made possible the surprise of October 6, 1973.

After 1973

In the present state of affairs, any hope for a move
toward a settlement lies with the Arabs' second school
of thought. Its open-endedness, leaving the door open
to join the first school, is a political problem of paramount importance with which Israeli diplomacy has to
wrestle. The problem is how to ensure that the first of
the two explanations of Egyptian open-endedness
alluded to earlier (pages 53–54), i.e., its being only an
insurance policy against Arab pressure, will come true
and not the second, i.e., its being mainly a tactic for
subsequently adding more demands. Some Israeli
leaders rushed to announce that Sadat opted for peace.
Their motivation in taking such a stance was commendable. However, by doing so they only played
into the hands of the Arab propaganda line that Israel
should withdraw without too much ado about security
arrangements. Unwittingly they thus supported legit-
imizing Egyptian open-endedness, thus causing damage to Israel's case.

On the other hand, it would not be good tactics for Israelis to attack open-endedness head-on by insinuating in a perfunctory fashion that Sadat's declaration—that he opted for a political settlement—should not be taken at its face value. Sadat is elegant in evading embarrassing questions, and his declarations have made a favorable impact on public opinion. Israel should exert its diplomatic efforts toward explaining the Egyptian position in depth. Only an understanding of the dangers of this open-endedness can elicit an appreciation of Israel's dilemma—and her demands. The thrust of Egyptian diplomacy is to blur, becloud, and fudge the open-endedness and its implications. The task for Israeli diplomacy is to bring it to light.

The Arabs can present their case in simplistic slogans. At most they have to try to conceal that their grievance, the redress of which in their version would be a matter of justice, is an *unlimited* grievance, which the opponent cannot redress to their liking and yet stay alive. Thus Israel's reluctance to abide by their demands is represented by them as only capricious, whereas actually it is an existential imperative.

Israel can effectively appeal only if its case is presented in analytical, intellectual, and historical terms. The same applies to its rebuttal of the Arab contentions. Israel's diplomatic pleadings can be successful only if they are not presented superficially, and if they project Arab ideological argumentation and are not limited to a discussion of day-to-day politics. For the

Israelis to present the Arab case in a fragmentary fashion cannot be convincing, as extreme Arab statements will be brushed aside by a public that is reluctant to take politicide at its face value. Israeli diplomacy can be convincing only if it presents the Arab position as a cohesive system of ideas, as it really is, demonstrating that politicide and its absolutist-totalistic nature are inherent in it. This may sound presumptuous on my part, yet I can't help feeling that Israeli diplomacy has yet to fully study its subject matter and do its homework.

The strong wish among diplomats to pose as practical people may be to compensate for their uneasiness that the main tools of their trade are word and persuasion. However, any interview of an Israeli diplomat with a foreign representative or a political leader is a missed opportunity if it deals only with current practical affairs, as the main problems between Israel and foreign governments lie not in the evaluation of current affairs. Israeli diplomacy should exert itself to explain the fundamentals of the conflict and, especially, analyze Arab attitudes in intellectual terms and in their implications for Israel.

Foreclosing the open-endedness of the second school cannot be achieved by Israel alone. It requires the support of public opinion, of governments, and first and foremost of the United States. That is why it is so crucial for Israel to gain international support by presenting a position that will appear reasonable to other nations.

The open-endedness will not be closed by benign tolerance of its ambiguities, but by urging clarity. Sadat should not be allowed to have it so easy, spreading facile noncommittal good tidings. He should be told that open-endedness in the conflict is untenable. If peace is, as he has said, for the next generation to decide, why should not withdrawal, too, be deferred? He has reiterated that he cannot agree to nonbelligerence without the fulfillment of Arab demands, as the Arabs would thereby lose their main means of pressure. By the same token, Israel cannot withdraw unless assured that withdrawal is part of a peace settlement that provides for the *end* of the conflict, i.e., that withdrawal would not entice an Arab onslaught.

Asad should be asked whether the resolutions of the 12th National Congress of the Ba'ath party bind him. Does he consider his demand for another Israeli withdrawal in the Golan as falling within the framework of the "Strategy of Phases" adopted by this Congress and which aims at bringing Israel to its demise gradually? If so, why does he think Israel should comply with such a demand?

The difficulty of inducing the Arabs to give up ideological positions may suggest another approach—that of step-by-step, practical settlements and interim agreements as a gradual incremental process of "interlocking" the rivals into positive arrangements which may make it more difficult for them to revert to open conflict and war. This approach has great appeal as a means of circumventing the ideological stumbling blocks. Such arrangements may have merit if their effects are *additive* in eroding the ideological positions, if mutual accommodations are thereby institutionalized, or if they constitute an irreversible *cumulative continuity*. Israelis may have justifiable apprehensions that all such settlements might boil down to depriving Israel of territorial assets which would be needed at a final stage in bargaining for a real settlement, without producing the hoped-for basic change in the Arab position, or that the "interlocking" might result in a one-sided "locking" of Israel, leaving the Arabs free to exert more pressure for advantages. The Sinai interim agreement of September 1975 is a case in point. Thus such a gradual approach might coincide with the Arabs' new approach of moderation in tactics and still maintain the fixity of their extreme strategic aim. Circumventing ideology might prove unattainable, as any political concession or any arrangement of a political nature would impinge on the Arabs' ideological stand.

Such a step-by-step arrangement is seen as satisfying the need to sustain "momentum." Momentum may be presumed to produce a feeling of suspension and expectancy on each side that things are moving in a favorable direction. However, momentum is not meant to be a process of weakening one side. Thus the momentum of Israel's withdrawals would not lead automatically to closing the open-endedness or to "interlocking" the rivals, forcing them to proceed on the path of mutual accommodation. Such weird metaphysical mechanics exist only in political folklore.

Some particular settlement or agreement might not necessarily be good and bring peace; it might be calamitous and bring war. The demand addressed to Israel to produce the miracles of "political momentum" may amount to pushing Israel to a precipice without setting up a fence. Israel's reluctance to comply is the result not of internal dissensions or the inability of its leadership to decide, but of the concrete impossibility of taking such a step as withdrawal on rational considerations. One should appreciate not only the difficulties of Sadat in the face of other Arabs, but the difficulty of Israel in being asked to make concessions without assurances.

The US should discuss the open-endedness issue with the Egyptians and Arabs in clear terms. Excessive considerateness toward their sensitivities may prove counterproductive. Egypt has not been pressed on its open-endedness as Israel has been pressed for "new ideas for political momentum."

What the Arabs seek from foreign public opinion, foreign diplomats, and governments is not an open endorsement of the politicidal objective, but merely a permissive tolerance toward its euphemistic expressions—"liberation," "return to their homes," "self-determination," "democratic secular state," "readiness to live with Jews," etc. It is difficult to find fault with such nice, humanistic expressions, and cumbersome to add the proviso "provided it means coexistence with Israel." But those things are exactly what have to be done. To refrain from reacting thus to these expressions, whatever the motivation—courtesy or the wish to treat Arabs' positions therapeutically—makes one a tacit partner in the politicidal objective. Westerners tend to give credence to what is said to them in private audiences, flattered to be made privy to someone's "true" attitude. In the Middle East, moderate whispers in foreign ears, if they are not repeated publicly, are worthless.

The Arabs were successful in getting the UN to adopt a series of resolutions which, according to Arab understanding, imply support of the politicidal stand, as they are interpreted as granting the Palestinians "the right" to establish their sovereignty over all of Palestine, including Israel. The UN General Assembly vote on November 10, 1975, condemning Zionism as a form of racism was, in Dr. Kissinger's words, "a moral condemnation of the state of Israel and not simply an abstract vote on Zionism." It was meant to subvert the moral basis for the state of Israel. It was thus a first step toward the endorsement of politicide.

The erosion of the politicidal attitude will come only through incessant castigation of it, and by impressing on the Arab publics and governments the odium that adherence to it, under whatever guise, will bring. Adherence to politicide is the Arab's main ideological weakness. Persuading the Arab leaders of the futility of their hope to confer legitimacy on their objective by presenting a seemingly pragmatic program is of paramount importance.

The same applies to the Palestinians and their verbal

pyrotechnics. Treating the Palestinians as if nobody knows what their objective is only encourages them to adhere to their present position of maximalist demands.[6] It does not leave the door open for them to make a change in their position, as the protagonists of such a policy may believe, but makes such a change unnecessary.

The question arises what would constitute a credible change in the Arab position. The Arabs went to such great lengths in denigrating Israel and calling for its demise that backing out of their position will not be easy. Their position became deeply ingrained in their nationalism so that announcing its change must have a "critical mass" to be of any effect. No single declaration can be expected to undo the cumulative weight of commitment to the traditional position. Thus a change has to be launched in a most conspicious, formal way. Changing a national position shared by the public has to be done in a fashion that will be recognized by the members of the collectivity and will influence them. Slick diplomatic formulas, incantations whispered in foreign ears, a mumble or a phrase in which the change is only implicit, would not do. A phrase that may imply a moderate attitude is worthless as a means of ushering in change if it is at the same time susceptible to a more extreme interpretation. For instance, "recognition of Palestinian self-determination in their homeland" is ambiguous, as homeland can mean either part of it or its entirety, the latter implying the demise of Israel. In order for a statement to deserve the adjective moderate or to signify a change, it should be unequivocal by excluding an extreme connotation.

No man and no political movement can be absolutely consistent in their utterings, and their position cannot be judged by one exceptional uttering, but by collating what attitude they took in the majority of cases. A real change in position can hardly be deduced from one statement, but can only be determined retrospectively by the outcome over time.

The PLO may try one day to modify its position or at least pose that its position has changed. For instance they may announce acceptance of Resolution 242 and drop "armed struggle" from the means of bringing about the democratic state as stipulated in the Twelfth National Council, and stop mincing words calling the "Palestinian authority" in the West Bank "a state." However so long as texts as the Covenant will be in force there is a possibility on falling back on them. The Covenant carries more weight than any resolution of the National Council or any announcement. Furthermore, Palestinians may contend, as they do now, that the General Assembly resolutions recognizing "Palestinians' self-determination" (with their politicidal meaning according to the Palestinians) carry more moral and political weight than the Security Council Resolution 242 and thus vitiate their acceptance of it.

Thus a change of the Palestinian and Arab position can be accomplished only by a whole series of clear declarations and actions, substantive and symbolic. It would have been much more comforting, but un-realistic, to think otherwise. Everything possible should be done to encourage the Arabs to make the change and to continue proceeding in the new course. A change must of course start with one first statement that should be heralded as a welcome beginning, not hailed as a consummate achievement. The absolutistic totalistic nature of the Arab and Palestinian position makes its relativization an onerous task indeed.

seven

The Question of
Israeli Concessions

The Need for Concessions

Winning public support has its price in concessions,
which Israel should declare its readiness to make. If
territory were to be given to the needy or according to
who requires it most for defense, or if international
"justice" had a distributive meaning, such as fairness in
regard to size of territory and its utilization, then a
very good case could have been made for allotting Israel the occupied territories, or a large portion of them.
This is not the way the world operates. However, the
international community gave its verdict in the form
of Security Council Resolution 242, the most favorable interpretation of which for Israel is that it should

withdraw to new lines that are more favorable to Israel than those of 1949–1967 but less favorable than the present ones. Israel cannot hope for a Helsinki, in which the accomplished territorial changes would be recognized. Thus Israel should reiterate its acceptance of Resolution 242, including the disbandment of settlements from the areas it would evacuate if the Arabs insist, as part of a peace agreement. The debate would then shift from the principle of withdrawal, yes or no, to the security conditions that would have to be satisfied as a *quid pro quo* for withdrawal. The Arabs could not claim that since these were their territories, they should be returned with no obligation on their part. They were taken because of aggressiveness on the Arabs' part which they are now reluctant to admit and would like the world to forget. Hence, these territories can only be returned after the Arabs have proved that the reasons for which they were taken no longer exist.

Establishing such proof is not simple, and is fraught with pitfalls. Verbal expressions of real readiness for peace finalizing the conflict, and acceptance of Israel as a permanent member of the Middle East, are of outstanding importance. Verbal commitments should entail a concrete content of arrangements, such as demilitarization, force limitations, *joint* Arab-Israeli supervision machinery, and gradual withdrawal over the years, and should be accompanied by a resolution for finalizing the conflict in the internal scene—political, social, and cultural. True, a settlement has to begin on the political level, but it has to be supported internally.

If inside the Arab states, in the schools, among the public, and on the part of the mass media, the old attitudes of describing Israel as a monstrosity remain, the political arrangement will be short-lived and will be subverted from underneath. Such changes in the climate of opinion cannot be accomplished overnight. At least there should be a manifest intention to produce them. A machinery to monitor such changes, despite the delicacy of the subject, can be devised.

Israel should declare its readiness to recognize the legitimate interests or rights of the Palestinians and to negotiate with the PLO, provided the Palestinians simultaneously recognize the legitimacy of Israel. Such a step would, as well, pass the burden of proof on to the Arabs and the Palestinians. One cannot be sanguine at all that the Palestinians are ready so far to make such a change in the core of their national doctrines. Their adherence to the unamended National Covenant of July 1968 testifies to this, as do the spirit and meaning of the resolutions of the National Councils and the many utterances of their leaders.

The contention that the PLO cannot recognize the legitimacy of Israel so long as Israel occupies the Arab territories is false if the territories occupied in 1967 are meant. Before their occupation, the PLO rejected any recognition of Israel. Nonrecognition and nonacceptance of Israel is a sacred dogma with the PLO, not a diplomatic gambit; it is a core value in PLO ideology, not a marginal proposition that can be easily discarded. In order to change its position toward acceptance of coexistence with Israel not one or a few articles of its National Covenant have to be amended but almost the whole document has to be rewritten.

So long as the PLO's central objective is the demise of Israel, Israel is in a morally unassailable position in refusing to recognize the PLO and negotiate with it, as such negotiation for the PLO can be only on the method of Israel's dismantlement. The only fault of such a policy is diplomatic, as Israel can gain at the international level from expressing readiness to recognize the PLO, even as a tactical exercise.

The sheer declaration by Israel of readiness to recognize and negotiate with the PLO might produce grave internal tensions and ruptures within the PLO. It would expose the extremism that is inherent in the PLO position. It might cause difficulties for the PLO vis-à-vis countries like Egypt. Not by accident did the resolution of the Twelfth Palestinian Council, convened in June 1974, include as a major guideline for the Palestinian movement the principles of no recognition and no conciliation. Israel's present policy of refusal to negotiate with the PLO shields the PLO from coming to grips with the political implications of its philosophy.

Justifiable as the Palestinian political claims for statehood may be, I consider an independent Palestinian state on the West Bank to be a historical impossibility, not because of economic unviability (the unviable can be made viable by assistance), but because of *geographical* considerations (it is landlocked and its need for an outlet through Jordan would give Jordan leverage over its destiny), and more so as a *demographic* imperative (its inhabitants and the Palestinians in Jordan would not agree to live in separate states). However, I consider that it has been a mistake on the part of Israel to present a historical evaluation as an Israeli political demand. Israel should not oppose the idea of such a state, but rather maintain sympathetic indifference toward it, the only proviso being that arrangements be made that it not serve as a firm base of attacks against Israel.

Such a state could not solve the acute problem of the Palestinians in Lebanon, or absorb them. It would elicit enmity from both its neighbors—Israel and Jordan—as basically it aspires to subvert them both.[1] It would not be big enough to satisfy the ambitions of the PLO leaders roving from one Arab capital to another, who would have to compete with the local leaders. The PLO leaders have so far had a vested interest in the conflict, which gives them international stature; they desire its continuation, not its resolution on less than their maximalist absolutist demands.

It seems to me that the PLO evaluation of the weakness of such a mini-state, on which it heaped appellations of abuse,[2] is closer to reality than the Israeli leaders' description of it as a time bomb. As such a bomb the Palestinian state would of course be the main victim of its explosion. Furthermore, Israel would have leverage over the Palestinian state by being able to control its passage to the Gaza strip.

By announcing its readiness to withdraw and let a Palestinian state be set up outside Israel's borders, Israel would return the Palestinian problem to its true natural habitat—inter-Arab politics—and free itself from a heavy burden. By its rejection of a West Bank Palestinian state, Israel has only served the Arab cause very substantially, as it has shielded the Arabs from their own devastating contradictions between Jordan and Palestine. Thus the nature of the regime in the West and East Banks—Hashemite or Palestinian—should be left to the self-determination of the population.

I do not see the Palestinization of Jordan in the offing. Jordan enjoys at present an economic boom, and its political entity is in a process of reinforcement and entrenchment, despite the Rabat conference or because of it, and with the active collaboration of its Palestinian population. It is not true that the future of Jordan is precariously dependent on the life of King Hussein. He has a competent brother. Furthermore, the Jordanian establishment and army have a vested interest in Jordan and will do their best to ensure the continuation of the regime.

The Palestinians' main thrust in their public relations is to enumerate their grievances and describe themselves as displaced people, deprived of a homeland. They capitalize on the association in people's minds between the idea of the absence of a Palestinian state and displacement. Their grievances are real, though the responsibility for them cannot be externalized only to others.[3] They refused a compromise solution. They started the civil war in 1948, and many of them were not banished, but left the country because of the disturbances and the war. From presenting true grievances they skip over to trying to make public opinion accept their solution of superseding Israel by a Palestinian Arab state, drawing attention to its positive aspects while omitting the negative results and suffering it would entail. This is a demagogic trick which can easily be exposed. Winning sympathy in the audience for one's misfortunes does not necessarily imply getting an endorsement for one's claims and solutions. No doubt it can be a step toward such an endorsement, a step which the Palestinians try to transform into a big leap, if their audience is not attentive to the difference.

The Palestinians present as an existential imperative the demand that all of former Palestine become their state. This is spurious. Arguing *ad hominem* they demand their human rights; arguing politically they clamor to enjoy their national rights. Political self-determination they can have in Jordan, the West Bank, and the Gaza strip. Against the Palestinians' claims that their problem can only be solved on the ruins of Israel as a Jewish state, Israel should present again a conciliatory plan of partition, juxtaposing Arab Palestinian absolutism with a relativist Israeli position. Both the Palestinians and the Israelis deserve national self-determination; thus the Palestinians' arrogation of rights—their claim that only they have rights of self-determination—can be exposed in all its chauvinistic ugliness.

It is not the fault of Israel that Jordan stays Jordanian, with the collaboration of its Palestinians who constitute about half its population, that many of them actively support the present Jordanian regime, or that the PLO fails to convert Jordan into a Palestinian state. Israel cannot do it for the Palestinians. Israel cannot compensate them for their failing by offering itself to them. Many Palestinians refuse to come under the Hashemite regime. Many others have shown loyalty to it. Anyhow, the Palestine hatred toward the Jordanian Kingdom is not an excuse for depriving the Israelis of their state.

Perhaps the Palestinians' failure to convert Jordan to Palestine despite their numbers (during 1949–1967 they constituted the majority in Jordan) is due to the fact that there is nothing singular or unique about them to differentiate them from the Jordanians, apart from some more hostility toward Israel. Both Jordanians and Palestinians share the same culture, religion, language, customs, etc. A change cannot be accomplished if the same features stay. At most such a change might mean the removal of the king which is a change in the regime, not in the entity.

The Eighth Palestinian National Council (February 28–March 4, 1971) announced that the Jordanians and Palestinians constitute "one people" and that Jordan and Palestine form one "territorial unity." It stated: "The creation of one political entity in Transjordan and another in Palestine would have no basis either in legality or as to the elements universally accepted as fundamental to a political entity. It would be a continuation of the operation of fragmentation by which colonialism shattered the unity of our Arab nation and the unity of our Arab homeland after the First World War."[4] It went on and explained (apologetically) that emphasizing the Palestinian distinction has been a temporary exigency. "The Palestinian revolution [i.e., the Palestinian movement and struggle] . . . acted in conformity with the exigencies of a specific historical stage, with the objects of concentrating on the direction of all forces towards Palestine so as to give prominence to our cause at Palestinian, Arab and international levels."[5] The "unity of the Jordanian and Palestinian fronts" is reiterated by all subsequent Palestinian National Councils. It is not a tactical device, but expresses the ethnic affiliation of the two groups.[6]

Paradoxically, the same position is taken by the Jordanian authorities in what may be called the "Jordanian Law of Return," stipulating that any Palestinian can secure Jordanian citizenship.[7] King Hussein has repeatedly declared that the Palestinians and Jordanians form one family. The competition between Jordan and the PLO is over who will swallow whom; there is no divergence as to the unity of the two parts or of the Palestinians and Jordanians.

All this is fraught with political consequences. If Jordan is part of the Palestinian homeland and the Jordanians and Palestinians are one people, then the Palestinians are not people in search of a homeland, but are simply desirous of *expanding a homeland they possess*. Almost two thirds of the Palestinians possess Jordanian citizenship. Furthermore, the Palestinians' participation in the political life of Jordan, occupying important posts in its government, is a manifestation of self-determination. Eventually, if the West Bank is federated with Jordan, the Palestinian element will predominate; thus the common state may become the "Palestine of tomorrow" (to use Arafat's expression in his speech at the UN General Assembly). This process can succeed only with Jordanian good will, but the present policy of the PLO in declaring its intention to subvert Jordan can only be self-defeating.

In their literature, Palestinian writers have boasted that they are the most pan-Arab group among the Arabs and that separatist deviations from Arab nationalism, namely ideologies like the Pharonic (in Egypt) and the Phoenician (in Lebanon), did not develop among them. When they need support or need to project strength, they stress their Arabness. When they claim Palestine, the Arab world is an alien area. Despite the ambivalencies between them and the other Arabs, they can have homes elsewhere, and many of them have been absorbed in Arab countries, speaking the same language and belonging to the same culture. From old Palestine hardly any names survived. The whole environment changed. Had they returned to it they would not "return to their homes," as their slogan goes, but would have to build new homes just as they would have to do elsewhere. When steps are taken to settle many thousands of Egyptian farmers in Iraq and the first contingent has already arrived there, why cannot some Palestinians—those who have not been absorbed—settle in Jordan and elsewhere in the Arab world?

Palestinian propagandists argue that not extending the Israeli Law of Return to them is an act of racial discrimination. Yet the Jewish immigrants come to build Israel, while the Palestinian Arabs would come to subvert it. And no country can be expected to collaborate on its demise.

Arab propagandists enjoy cataloguing the sins of Israel. Many are false, some are true. Israel, in order to preserve itself, is driven by Arab hostility sometimes to act in a way that cannot be measured by the criteria of absolute morality. Human imperfection demands viewing things in relative perspective. Arabs and Palestinians apply double standards of morality, judging Israel as it is, and Arab countries and Palestinian behavior as they ideally should be. Compared with Arab behavior, Israel's towers sky-high. Jews were hanged in public squares in Iraq to the mirth of the mob. Palestinian Arabs were hanged in both Syria and Egypt. Despite provocations Israel has not applied capital punishment even to those implicated in the most horrendous murders. The same applies to its Arab minority. The fact is that Jewish life in the Arab world became insufferable and most Jews left, while in Israel there thrives a large Arab community. This fact speaks eloquently. The common Arab argument that the Jews emigrated from Arab countries because of Zionist machinations is frivolous.

Readiness to offer concessions—to withdraw, to disband settlements, to recognize the Palestinians, etc.— is, in my opinion, either a tactical step or a strategic position, depending on Arab reaction. If the Arabs refuse to finalize the conflict in a fashion that will give Israel reasonable assurances for its security, then the offer of all these concessions is *tactical* as a means of improving our political position to withstand future ordeals. If the Arabs are ready for peace, it becomes a major *strategic* policy.

The previous analysis of the three Arab schools of thought holds only meager hope for the second eventuality.

Objections

There are very cogent arguments against this policy of concessions. Israel's declaring its readiness to withdraw and let a Palestinian state be established would, in all probability, result in the Arab states' and the United States' taking Israel at its word and exerting pressure on it to act accordingly, without the fulfillment of its security demands. The interim agreement of September 1975 is a case in point; although Israel withdrew and gave up the Sinai strategic passes and the oil fields without an Egyptian political *quid pro quo,* Egypt did no more than serve notice of its acceptance of these areas.

Furthermore, there are objective difficulties in making the security safeguards concrete and real. A declaratory dovish stance would prove to be a trap. Israel's concessions would be fractionized, and its refusal to concede in any individual case would be described as petty, narrow-minded obstinacy, inciting public opinion and governments against it, whereas the demands from the Arab side are not divisible and thus are less prone to pressures and "salami tactics." Israel's withdrawal would be irreversible, for by withdrawing it would lose strategic assets, whereas the Arabs' actions, even in their far-reaching meaning—the undertaking to finalize the conflict and change the internal climate of opinion—would be easily reversible and might be only sham. It would be an exchange of tangibles for intangibles, of real property that could not be recovered for a promise that could be revoked. The plurality of the Arab actors, the pressure of the extremists who would not accede to the agreement, and the impossibility of burying all the bones of contention and settling all residual disputes could all exert pressure on the Arabs to reopen the conflict. They might not be able to resist such a temptation once Israel had weakened itself by withdrawal. These are precisely the arguments of the first Arab school of thought (and perhaps of the second) as to why a settlement is not dangerous for the Arabs and would not result in a freeze.

The big powers and especially the United States will exert pressure on Israel to show understanding of Arab sensitivity and will accept an Arab obligation to finalize the conflict even if it is couched in vague equivocal terms. The big powers will argue that to agree categorically to finalizing the conflict may seem to the Arabs to be an unacceptable repudiation of their traditional position—which has become an important tenet enshrined in Arab national thought—and an ignominious surrender. Arab leaders acceding to such a firm obligation would not be able to face their public. Thus the door for the continuation of the conflict will be left wide open even on the formal official level. At most such an obligation to terminate the conflict will be a verbal ploy.

For instance, suppose the PLO realizing the absurdity of its absolutist position and under the impact of its reverses in Lebanon convenes a new National Council which decides in some vague formula to recognize Israel, accept coexistence, though without giving up the "vision" of a unitary Palestinian state and the right to achieve it even if by peaceful means. Can Israel accept it? Can we discard our experience with PLO formulas? By no means.

Moreover, internal difficulties in Arab societies, the difficulties of adjustments of their culture to modern life, and possible social upheavals and revolutions might drive them to external adventures. Pent-up pressures in Arab societies, factions seething with desires for vengeance, the cruelty in the Arabs' internecine wars,[8] treachery in inter-Arab politics (the PLO and Syrians from allies become cruel enemies)—all these augur ill for a modicum of moderation toward so deeply hated a neighbor as Israel. A future Arab government might renege on the obligations of its predecessor. Thus it is better for Israel to sit tight and risk the disapproval of world public opinion and governmental censure, while it does its best to explain its case and predicament; to exist, even under the hardships of being besieged, abandoned, and isolated from support, rather than to be nice, affable, forthcoming, reasonable—and perish.

This is a formidable argument, and one that will get greater support among the Israeli public the greater the pressure on Israel to make one-sided concessions without getting assurances. It is now the *pièce de résistance* of the more extreme circles in Israel, within both the government and the opposition. They are pessimistic about Israel's possibilities of withstanding Arab pressures or an Arab military onslaught once Israel withdraws, especially from the West Bank.

Conclusion

Few countries in history have lived against such odds, facing so many adversities, as does Israel. It is not easy to live and raise children in a country faced with the vision of a future of continuous strife. No doubt there are grave dangers in the line of policy here proposed, and these have to be faced by Israel and to be considered very seriously by the West, especially by the public and government of the United States. If Israel withdraws and war comes as a result, the odds it will have to face will increase. Israel will fight back gallantly, with great resourcefulness, and such a war would cause tremendous losses and ruin. What is at stake is neither a territorial settlement nor a controversy over borders, but the sheer existence of Israel. The moral havoc the destruction of Israel would wreak on Western civilization should be realized. It is no good evading these unthinkables. They should be addressed squarely.

Despite all these considerations, it is my personal conviction that for Israel to declare its readiness to make the concessions enumerated is the best policy. Its merits and faults can be better gauged when compared with the other major political alternatives that Israel might pursue.

eight

Three Israeli Schools
of Thought

Israel is extremely heterogeneous in its ideas for the solution of its political problems. Yet for the sake of brevity I shall simplify the political range of opinions, again into three distinct schools of thought. These schools of thought are not an imaginative abstraction, but are representative of the national debate now going on in Israel. Their conceptualization as three schools is mine. They are all *reactive;* i.e., their policy prescriptions are derivative of or deduced from their assumptions about the Arab position and threats. Therefore I shall present them in the form of an equation, the first part of which is their characterization of the Arab position and the second part their prescription for the Israeli response.

ISRAEL'S POLICY

The "Dovish-Dovish" School

This school starts from the assumption that the Arab
position has become more lenient and that there are
influential circles in the Arab world that desire to live
in peace with Israel and that have given up the politicidal objective, even if they have difficulties in ac-
knowledging this publicly. It is alive to the dangers of
the continuation of the conflict for Israel and has a
genuine, strong urge for peace, which predisposes it
to inflate the significance of ambiguous signs of Arab
moderation, to present dissident weak voices of moderation as if they are dominant and to play down signs
of the Arabs' harsh positions. It treats with impatience
anyone who points to Arab extremism or any research
of the conflict that proves Arab intransigence. Israelis,
it says, should preoccupy themselves with peace and
its blessings and not the conflict.

Israel should take a dovish stand by offering concessions, by offering to withdraw, by recognizing the
Palestinians, and by being ready to negotiate with the
PLO. Such concessions will bring dovish responses
from the Arab side. If the position of the Arabs is not
at present exactly dovish, it is dovish in the making,
potentially dovish, a tendency which Israeli dovishness can bring to fruition. Dovishness on both sides,
mutually reinforcing itself, will culminate in peace as
the ultimate termination of the conflict.

Credulity about Arab actual or potential dovishness
makes this school ready to offer its concessions lavishly

without too much ado about security arrangements, almost to the point of unilateralism. It tends to downgrade the importance of the territorial element in Israeli strategic thinking. Hence it considers the conclusion of peace agreements as rather a simple business and treats with some impatience the problems of how to ensure Israel security. It does not deny that such problems exist, yet it is inclined to belittle their significance in face of Arab peaceful intentions and Israeli proven military superiority. Being pacifist by temperament, this school, ironically, takes pride in Israeli military valor which constitutes a component in its dovishness. This school is thus willing to take strategic risks.

The central tenet of this school is that the key to peace is in the hands of Israel and in its changing its policy. Thus the blame for the continuation of the conflict and the absence of peace also devolves on Israel. This accusation is implied in the statements of spokesmen of this school even if they do not always articulate it.[1] Thus, unwittingly, this school has helped the Arabs' public relations both in depicting Israel as intransigent, as constituting the main obstacle to peace, and in presenting the Arabs as much more moderate than reality warrants. It is difficult to gauge how far this school has contributed to some tilting of the scales in many circles of public opinion in a direction favorable to the Arabs.

An accusation direct or indirect that Israel could have achieved peace and has failed because of territorial demands undermines the moral basis of the government and state of Israel, inasmuch as it implies depravity in not valuing peace above material gains. It may have demoralizing effects internally, with its implication that in their territorial ambitions the political leaders have become callous to the lives of the younger generation which would be sacrificed in wars caused by their intransigence.

I do not doubt the idealistic good intentions of this school. But paradoxically its moral tenor drives it to the immorality of employing double standards in judging the behavior of the contestants. It is more lenient in its judgment of Arab behavior, more stringent in judging Israeli behavior. Starting with self-criticism before criticizing the opponent is commendable in that charity begins at home. The problem arises in that after criticizing Israel this school stops, and a slanted picture emerges. That there are Jews supporting the Arabs in castigating the Jewish state serves as trenchant proof that Arab condemnation of Israel has substance.

The picture will be deficient if I do not add that the existence of this group serves to create, as well, a favorable impression of Israel abroad. That is to say, the Israelis are not all intransigent and nationalistic, and the government is a true democracy since it tolerates such harsh dissension and criticism. On balance, however, it is my impression that the negative effect outweighs the positive.

The "dovish-dovish" school tends to accept at face value the Palestinians' claims that they constitute "a people," including the authenticity and historicity of their peoplehood and its uniqueness. The Palestinians, therefore, must have a state of their own as the in-carnation of their singularity. It argues that such a state in the West Bank and the Gaza strip will satisfy the Palestinians, and Israel should help them to bring it into being. Henceforth the Palestinians will live peacefully with Israel.

Its pro-Palestinian orientation produces a propensity to consider the Palestinians and Israelis as eventual allies against the Arab states. Israel should thus sup-port the Palestinians against the other Arabs. Unwit-tingly it considers Arab hostility to Israel as autono-mous from the Palestinian issue. Hence, despite its declaration that the Palestinian issue is the core of the conflict, it sees other bones of contention almost over-shadowing it.

The extremities of the PLO and its absolutism do not worry this school of thought, as it contends that a dovish attitude by Israel will ensure that the moderates among the Palestinians will prevail. Being impressed with Palestinian nationalism, it tends to downgrade the vigor of Jordanian nationalism. Thus it disposes of the problem of the Jordanian entity by readiness to sacri-fice Jordan on the Palestinian altar. Since it views a Palestinian state in the West Bank as politically viable, it tends to refrain from delving into the problem of the relationship between it and Jordan. Possibly such over-sight is due to forebodings that to consider this prob-lem might be to nibble at the assumption of the via-bility of the Palestinian state.

The idealistic temperament of the adherents of this

school of thought is expressed in their philosophy of life and their perspective on international relations. They tend to be liberal, progressive, believers in the UN and its role, and supporters of *détente*. International conflicts are all solvable if people of "good will" from both sides are resolved to find a settlement. Human rationality is bound to prevail. Thus all international actors are interested in settling the Arab-Israeli conflict, including the Soviet Union.

This school of thought has great merit in having *internal consistency*—dovishness on both sides of the equation. Apparently, because of the idealistic temperament of its members, or their simplicity, they need such a consistency else they would suffer uneasiness from cognitive dissonance. Inconsistency may seem to this school to be dishonest trickery. Thus the development of its ideas is dialectical; from discerning dovish symptoms in the Arab position it comes to propose a dovish policy for Israel, and its advocacy of a dovish Israeli policy produces an urge to conceive dovishness on the Arab side, as an insurance that an Israeli dovish policy will meet with Arab acceptance.

Its flaw is in the incongruence of the first part of the equation with reality—since its facile assumption of Arab dovishness is false. The members of this school are predisposed to excessive "voluntarism"—giving prominence to their will to see Arab moderation as the dominating trend, downgrading the external reality that is incongruent with their conceptions. This contradiction is too obvious to the Israeli public, and therefore this school cannot be persuasive to Israelis and is condemned to remain a minority.

The "Hawkish-Hawkish" School

This school holds that the Arab position is at present unalterably hawkish and thus concludes that Israel too has to adopt a hawkish position by holding the occupied areas, particularly in the West Bank and on the Golan Heights, as withdrawal would weaken Israel's strategic position, inviting an Arab attack. All safeguards are bound to be flimsy in the face of the basic Arab hostility to the existence of the Israeli state; only territory can ensure some margin of security. Had the Arabs shown they really desired peace, proponents of this school sometimes avow, withdrawal could be considered. However, given the present state, withdrawal would be suicidal. The development of military technology requires that Israel continue to maintain control of the West Bank in order that Israeli population centers not be at the mercy of Arab governments or even of guerrilla bands roaming the West Bank. The national airport, Lod, could easily be paralyzed from the Judean mountains.

Holding a political position that is mostly derivative from or responsive to the rival's challenges holds some inconveniences, since the position tends to become subordinate and reactive. Thus the nationalist vigor of this school has compelled it to present a position that is autonomous, assuming the attitude of a plaintiff and eschewing the apologetics of a defendant. It presents a claim to the West Bank as part of historical Israel and the "historical rights" of Jews to the Holy Land. Pragmatic considerations of security and historical, ideological, and religious memories merge in a symbiosis in which pragmatism is abetted by ideology. Thus this school transcends the existential Zionism that typifies the first school and the third, "hawkish-dovish" school, i.e., their defensive position of preserving the achievements of the Zionist enterprise, and goes over instead to a vindictive type of Zionism. Toward its Israeli detractors it argues that demurring from claiming rights to Nablus or Hebron might vitiate Israel's right to Haifa and Tel Aviv.

The claim of "historical rights" as a major guiding principle embroils this school in a difficult position vis-à-vis the Palestinians who lived in the country, as if their stay has been temporary and illicit during the absence of its legitimate proprietor—the Jew—and now that he has returned they have to restore his property to him. However, this claim is made only on the collective or national level, for in a compensatory fashion members of this school repeatedly present themselves as staunch protagonists of the Palestinians' civil rights as citizens of a Jewish state.

The "hawkish-hawkish" school demands the annexation of the West Bank to Israel and the application of Israeli law there. (Until now the Jordanian law holds sway in the West Bank.) It downgrades the apprehension that incorporating a large Palestinian community of about 600,000 Palestinian Arabs in Israel would dilute its Jewish nature. With a penchant for analogical reasoning it argues that in the past the ratio between Jews and Arabs was worse, and still Zionism was not disheartened. Jewish immigration, it tries to persuade itself, will counterbalance the worsening of the population distribution.

It calls for settling the West Bank mainly in areas that would not require displacement of Arabs. Even if such Jewish settlements do not affect the predominantly Arab character of the area, they have a symbolic value. Banning Jews from living or settling in the West Bank, the school maintains, is an absurdity. Why should Jews be allowed to live in New York and prohibited from living in their historical homeland!

This school challenges the authenticity of the Palestinian phenomenon. Even the name of the Palestinians is problematic, as etymologically it comes from the Philistines, to whom the Palestinian Arabs do not relate historically or culturally, nor do they derive any inspiration from them. Apart from the Jewish period Palestine has never existed as a political entity such that feelings of uniqueness and identification could have developed among its inhabitants. The Arabs on the shores of the Mediterranean, some protagonists of this school even argue, are basically imperialist intruders who bursting from the Arabian peninsula disrupted violently the old pattern of peoples who lived there. The Palestinian Arabs are basically Arabs, having no historical or cultural features to distinguish them from

the neighboring Arab communities. During the Ottoman period, up to 1917, Palestine was divided into
districts that were amalgamated with other areas in
Lebanon, Syria, and Trans-Jordan. The Arabs in these
areas identified themselves as Muslims, Arabs, or
Ottomans or by their village or town. It was only the
British who carved out Palestine, and during their rule
up to 1948 the term "Palestinian" merely signified citizenship namely, the kind of passport one possessed,
and applied to all those who resided in the territory.[2]
The "hawk-hawks" use this argument, which in itself is
unassailable, to belittle the importance of the Palestinian national movement or its claims to nationhood.
They vehemently oppose the setting up of a Palestinian state in the West Bank, for both security and historical considerations. In their view, such a Palestinian
state, because its weakness would be a source of in-
stability, might even become a Soviet base.[3]

Circles in this school of thought advocate allotting
Jordan to the Palestinians and the PLO. Let the Palestinians set up their state there, and let Israel help in
achieving it. Thus the Palestinian problem would be
settled once and for all.

Their view of international relations is a cynical,
jaundiced realism. The international arena is a continuous power struggle, where arguments of morality
and justice have limited weight. Thus an attempt by
Israel to present a reasonable, moderate, moral position would be futile. Arab oil counts for more than a
thousand persuasive arguments. Furthermore, the

claim of the Jews to their land has in itself moral validity of a high historical significance.

Ideologically and politically this school is anti-Soviet. It sees the clash between East and West, and in particular between the US and the Soviet Union, as deep and real. Israel is an asset for the West in this struggle. This belief alleviates for this school the severity of the divergence in attitudes and policies between the US and Israel, and leads it to believe that Israel, because of its importance, can allow itself to resist US pressure to offer concessions.

The school's attitude toward the possibility of war is one of heroic fatalism. In either case, whether Israel withdraws or refuses to withdraw, the Arabs will seek an opportunity to launch war. In the first case, it would be in order to benefit from Israel's weakened position; in the second, they would be more hesitant as Israel's strategic position would be stronger. This school argues emphatically that if there is a possibility to prevent war it lies with the present strategic borders which may discourage the Arabs from initiating hostilities. Still, the Arabs may try to isolate Israel from external support and start hostilities. The possibility of war as almost a foregone conclusion reduces the forebodings of war. The school is thus resigned to the idea of war and its members tend to show preparedness for sacrifice and heroism.

This school of thought attaches great importance to factors such as qualitative superiority in morale, devotion, fortitude of spirit in deciding the outcome of wars.

Thus it is a great believer in Israel's ability to withstand the pressure of the conflict and prevail.

Despite considering the Arabs' position as hawkish, the "hawkish-hawkish" school harbors the hope that eventually they will become resigned not only to Israel's existence but to its conquests, for, even with these added areas, Israel is insignificantly small compared with the overall vastness of Arab territories. Turbulence, upheavals, and revolutions in Arab societies will teach the Arabs that their real problems lie elsewhere and not in the confrontation with Israel and thus cause them to be more conciliatory toward Israel.

A strong argument of this school is that the absolutist-totalistic nature of the Arab position excludes Arab satisfaction by less than the demise of Israel. The position's lack of elasticity means that Arab rejection of Israel does not diminish as Israel's stand becomes more conciliatory. The values of this rejection are constant and are not at all a function of Israel's size. A smaller Israel is as much an anathema in Arab eyes as a bigger one. The Arabs refused to make peace before 1967, and the area occupied in the war has not made them more moderate and forthcoming. Israel's doves only delude themselves that they can placate Arab hostility by concessions. The real gap that thwarted an agreement was that between the moderates of both sides. Even declaring readiness to withdraw as a gesture, as the third Israeli school proposes, is flimsy as a political measure. Politics are made of hard facts, not some fake, dandy histrionics of posing as moderate.

Peace cannot be bought as long as there is no readiness for it on the Arab side.

Summing up, this school, as does the first one, enjoys the advantage of *internal consistency* in its equation, i.e., a congruity between diagnosis and prognosis. By giving recognition to the Arabs' harsh position toward Israel, this school is able to command larger Israeli public support than the first school. Furthermore, it represents a streak of national vitality and a devotion to national aspirations (which the first school sometimes denigrates as "myths"). This too strengthens its popular appeal. Thus when an Israeli criticizes this school, he has to be cautious about not sounding as if he were encouraging defeatism. On the other hand, by its excessive national vindictiveness this school harms the Israeli image abroad. Furthermore, its vindictiveness may help somehow to exonerate the Arab position of blame for its absolutist-totalistic nature, as analogies may be drawn between extremism on the two sides.

This school's main weakness lies in not offering an incentive to the Arabs to desire mutual accommodation with Israel. Its conditions may sound to them as a demand for unconditional surrender.

Another flaw of the "hawkish-hawkish" school lies in the incongruity between the second half of the equation and international reality. Can Israel allow itself to maintain a hawkish stand and refuse to withdraw, inasmuch as most of the states in the world, including the United States, demand a withdrawal? This school's belief in Israel's strategic utility to the US in world politics blurs its sight so that it cannot appreciate this difficulty. Thus this school, like the "dovish-dovish" school, manifests a voluntarist tendency, in this case, in trying to see international reality as it wishes to see it, believing that Israel can influence world public opinion and the positions of governments, bringing them to agree with Israeli conquests.

There is a difference, however, between the first and second schools' incongruities with reality. The first school's incongruity is between its *description* and the Arab reality; the second school's is between its *prescription* and the international reality. One can make the evaluation that the discrepancy of the second school is less rigorous, as a prescription is more a question of opinion than is a description.

The "Hawkish-Dovish" School

This school advocates the policy that I proposed and elaborated upon in Chapter 7. In a sense it is not a school, as there is no political party behind it, and may as well, therefore, be termed a conception. It tries to be stringently reality-oriented in both parts of the equation, recognizing both the harshness of the Arab position and the exigencies of international reality.

It suffers from a grave deficiency in its lack of internal consistency in advocating a dovish policy in the face of Arab extremism. However, this inconsistency, or dissonance, reflects the complexity of the Israeli existential predicament. The inconvenience of having to tackle inconsistencies on the intellectual level is preferable to harboring gratifying inconsistencies with reality. Politics is the art of managing inconsistencies. The only way to control them is by first bringing them to consciousness.

Historically, this conception represents the continuity in Zionist policy from British Mandate times, as the mainstream of Zionism tried to take up conciliatory positions, thus maneuvering the Arabs into making extreme, nonconciliatory demands. (The historical roots of the first school are in the Brith-Shalom movement and the Ihud; the second school stems from the old Revisionist movement.)[4]

This third school, like the second, challenges the authenticity and historicity of the Palestinian phenomenon. Yet it draws different conclusions, contending that practically it is immaterial whether the Palestinians have historical roots or not. What is important is that many of them by now have a strong feeling of identification and affiliation. Nations constitute themselves, as the French philosopher Ernest Renan observed, by a daily plebiscite. Thus if a group of people claim they are a nation, they are so by the fact that they claim it.

The school's international-relations outlook is half way between those of the first and the second schools. Man is a complicated animal. In making external policy he seeks his own happiness and interests, yet still is moved by ethical considerations. That is why this school has put a high premium on the need to justify Israeli behavior in the eyes of public opinion.

Whereas the first and second schools are mainly concerned with strategy and final objectives, the third school deals with tactics, which are in this case flexible, capable of leading to a strategy of peace if the Arabs agree to move toward the finalization of the conflict, or, if they persist in their present position, which is the more probable case, toward a strategy of the long haul in the continuation of the conflict. The third school is not at all a disguised effort to hold the occupied territories on the pretext that the Arabs will reject peace. It genuinely would prefer peace to anything else if peace were possible.

An important virtue of the third school is its relativism, in terms of its conciliatory attitude, seeing the conflict as a clash between genuine national aspirations and true grievances.

Since the Six-Day War Israel has suffered severely from fragmentation of its national consensus, and this has stalemated policy making. The third school might enable Israel to extract itself from the deadlock, since, being midway between the other schools, it could serve as a meeting ground for them. The spokesmen of the first school ("dovish-dovish") admit that their readiness to withdraw is conditional, predicated on Arab acceptance of arrangements that would secure the safety of Israel, and many spokesmen of the second school ("hawkish-hawkish") declare that for a "real" peace they are ready to withdraw. Thus the distances between these two schools and the third one can be narrowed down. Both the first and second schools might still converge on the position of the third from different perspectives and different approaches. For the first school, concessions advocated by the third school might be considered a *strategic* step, while the second school might consider them to be only *tactical.*[5]

For the first school such a step would be easy, as it does not require a major change in its policy prescription. For the second school it would be much more difficult; this school might be agreeable only if convinced that Israel's offering concessions would not be seized upon by the big powers—and in particular the US—to force Israel to withdraw without political concessions and assurances from the Arab side. Thus the mellowing of the second school is dependent on the US showing understanding toward Israel's strategic forebodings. American political behavior has not always helped develop conciliatory trends in Israel. Cajoling or coercing the Israeli government to sign the recent Sinai interim agreement without a political *quid pro quo,* it is my impression, contributed to strengthening of the second school within the Israeli public.

Also, the second Israeli school might add the proviso that the proposal to withdraw will be limited in time and that if the Arabs are not ready to terminate the conflict there is no sense in Israel's abstention from settling some of the occupied areas of strategic importance. The occupied areas are not a deposit to be kept on a long-term basis and then returned to the owners with compound interest. If the Arabs are not ready to make peace, then preparation for war is mandatory for Israel as the sole policy, which will include settling these areas to strengthen Israel's hold. Such a settlement policy would not be unprovoked annexationism, but would be a reaction to Arab hostility.

Recognition of the Palestinians' national rights is difficult for the second school; nevertheless this difficulty too can be overcome, as the tendency within the school to Palestinize Jordan implies in principle such a recognition.

The Israeli government's policy calling for what it terms "a territorial compromise" is flexible enough to enable reconciliation with the third school. Taking into consideration the extremities of the Arab position, the nature of the politicidal objective, the important role of the ideological structures concerning the conflict in Arab nationalism, cultural life, literature and education, one can argue that a change of the Arab position should be signaled not only by a promise on paper but also by agreeing that Israel would improve its territorial position by "defensible borders." Many Israelis are convinced that such a demand is justified and feel that the Arabs owe it to them. The acid test for an Arab change of position and heart is readiness to meet Israel's territorial security sensitivities.

There is another argumentation of a practical order. Arab acceptance of coexistence with Israel came reluctantly under the pressure of their realization that they could not achieve their objective. It was not a spiritual conversion but coercion of circumstances. Hence, circumstances permitting, they may revert to their old position. Only territorial changes and the establishment of defensible boundaries can serve as some kind of a hedge against such a eventuality. The boundaries may even be related to the "quality" or the "intensity" of the peace arrangements and the kind of environment they will create—small withdrawal for a "negative peace" of lack of violence, greater withdrawal for a "positive peace" of commercial, cultural and diplomatic exchanges.

I have not dealt with the territorial problems and Jerusalem in specific terms, as at the present stage the emphasis should be on Israel announcing readiness to offer concessions and to recognize and negotiate with the PLO. Not only has the present Israeli policy enabled the protagonists of the second Arab school to hide behind seemingly moderate programs of action. Also, the refusal to announce readiness to withdraw has spared the Arabs from articulating their objective, thus helping them in the main thrust of their position, which is to acquire legitimacy for their objective under the guise of the legitimacy achieved for their program of action, or, more precisely, to mask the absolutist-totalistic nature of their position by a guise of relativism. Israel's case is good, yet the present political stand weighs heavily on it and condemns Israel to tortuous apologetics, instead of enabling it to come up with a clear case and throw the gauntlet to the Arabs.

A firm but moderate stand by Israel would counteract precisely this Arab attempt to gloss over the objective by means of the moderate program. Exposure of Arab extremism would justify the demand for an Arab political *quid pro quo* for Israel's withdrawal. The Arab plan for incremental reduction of Israel to a condition of demise would be challenged by the need to agree beforehand on the modality of coexistence between both sides. The implementation would start after the agreement.

For Israel to adopt a moderate "relativist" stance is very important morally for the Israelis themselves and especially so for the younger generation. Perseverance in the face of the ordeals awaiting them is dependent on the conviction that everything possible has been done by Israel to prevent war, and that the blame for it, if it comes, lies with the nonconciliatory attitude of the Arabs.

The prescription of the third school is not perfect, and it is replete with dangers. Its validity can be judged in only a comparative fashion, by assessing the relative advantages and disadvantages of the prescriptions of the three Israeli schools. I submit that the others' shortcomings are graver. In politics the choice is often not between good and evil, but between bad and worse. Still the dilemmas are awesome, as the sheer existence of the state is dependent on such a decision. First and foremost each of the three schools sets out to secure the existence of Israel, yet because of the complexities of the situation each arrives at a different solution.

It is easy to find fault with each of the schools of thought or to demonstrate that they all lead to blind alleys. In such a situation the preferable line of action is one that leads to a position that will be tenable for a longer time and where the waiting is more tolerable. This is one of the virtues of the third school.

The third school enjoys an advantage over the other two schools considering the dynamics of the conflict and the possible influence of each of the schools on the Arab position. The idealism of the first school in its unwary alacrity to offer concessions may court disaster. The rigidity and vindictiveness of the second school would estrange world public opinion and reinforce Arab extremism, serving for them as proof that their imagery of Israel as expansionist is true.

Hopes for an improvement and eventual settlement lie with the third school. Its adoption as policy would improve Israel's international stance. Such an improvement in its turn may eventually impress the Arabs with the need to finalize the conflict in a contractual peace and reach permanent coexistence.

The complexity of the third school is a disadvantage. Its internal inconsistency may even arouse opposition, especially in a democratic regime in which the issues generally have to be presented to the public in simplistic terms as clearcut issues and straightforward solutions. Its proposals cannot be sloganized. People may be bewildered and look askance at this strange combination of attributing hawkishness to the rival and nevertheless advocate a dovish policy, considering such a policy an unnatural transplantation or grafting. Understanding the utility of such a policy requires a degree of sophistication. For it to become a rallying point for the diverse views in Israel requires preparatory work and respected leaders explaining to the Israelis the advantages of such a policy.

The similarity between the dovish prescriptions of the first and third schools is only partial and formal. Believing in Arab good intentions and their possible moderation the first school's dovish proposals are cavalier. Having a ginger skeptical view of Arab moderation the third school's dovish proposals are strictly conditional and guarded to a point of almost not deserving the adjective dovish. What is more important, the objectives each of these schools sets out to attain are different. The first school proposes dovishness as a means to achieve peace, whereas for the third it is meant to improve Israel's international standing. The third school tries to endow Israel's diplomacy with subtlety and thus to redress an imbalance attributed by some influential circles to Israel between its military adroitness and diplomatic ineptitude. The first school maintains that a dovish policy by Israel will elicit a dovish Arab response; the third school does not entertain such a hope. The first school castigates the Israeli government for immorality, for valuing annexation of territory as more precious than peace. The third does not indulge in the illusion that a more lenient Israeli policy will bring peace; its criticism is that Israeli policy is ill-advised. It blames Israel not for immorality, but for a lack of sagacity and lack of realism in not improving its stance. Both the first and third schools are relativist in their approaches, taking into consideration the adversary claims, and are not only preoccupied with Israel's crude self-interests. The relativism of the third school is more balanced; the first school is idealistically lopsided almost to a point of self-negation. Furthermore, the first school belittles the grievances of the Arabs and the Palestinians by considering them easy to be satisfied. It does not view them in their full human and political stature. Its tendency to disregard harsh Arab statements on their position and on their demands may even imply contempt.[6]

There are similarities as well between the second and third schools, particularly in their starting points and objectives. They share the belief that a solution to the conflict is not in the offing. Both aim at strengthening Israel to face future challenges. They diverge on the issue of how this can be achieved—by securing territories, as the second school maintains, or by winning international support, as the third school hopes.

The differences between the three schools are highlighted in Table 3.

TABLE 3: DIFFERENCES BETWEEN THE THREE ISRAELI SCHOOLS

	Dovish-Dovish	Hawkish-Hawkish	Hawkish-Dovish
Evaluation of Arab positions	Israeli dovishness will elicit a dovish Arab response	Arab hawkishness is due to unalterable Arab nationalism and maliciousness	Hawkishness is too deeply ingrained in Arab ideology to lapse easily
Policy prescription	Dovish policy by Israel will bring peace	Israel should sit tight and refuse withdrawal, mainly for security considerations but for ideological reasons too; annexations	Dovish policy will primarily give Israel better international standing, required for better withstanding the conflict, which will continue
Perspective on the future	Peace	Continuation of the conflict	Continuation of the conflict
Tactics and strategy	Dovishness by Israel is a strategy	Hawkishness is a strategy	Dovishness is primarily tactics, becoming strategy if Arabs agree to terminate the conflict, which is improbable
Projected change in Arab attitude	Predicated on dovish Israeli policy	Eventually Arabs will resign themselves to Israel's existence and to its conquests; annexation is compatible with peace	Change is dependent on historical circumstances and the world's condemnation of politicide; Israel's holding to occupied areas aggravates Arab position
Territory vis-à-vis international support	Question does not arise since possibility of peace is in the offing	International support is unreliable, fickle; territory is more important	International—especially US—support and supplies are crucial

	Dovish-Dovish	Hawkish-Hawkish	Hawkish-Dovish
Role of ideology	Ideologically motivated; people are good and peace-loving	Strong Zionist motivation; withdrawal impinges on basic rights of the Jews to Israel	Pragmatic; appreciative of idealism of first school and national vigor in second
Strength of school	Congruity between assessment of Arab position and prescription for Israel	Congruity between assessment of Arab position and prescription for Israel; repository of national vitality and readiness to sacrifice	Consistency as to Arab position and international reality; adoption of its policy can increase support for Israel
Weakness of school	Incongruity between image of Arab position and Arab reality; idealizes Arab position	Incongruity between policy prescription and international reality; possibility of peace on its terms very remote; produces an image of Israel intransigence	Internal inconsistency between assessment of Arab position and prescription; need to resist pressure to make concessions without assurances
Effect on world public opinion	Creates favorable impression that not all Israelis are hawkish but government is; helps Arabs to pose as moderates; joins with them in condemning Israel	Mostly unfavorable; gives impression of Israel as nationalistic and expansionalistic; does, however, show national vitality	Favorable in US and West; adoption of moderate policy will improve Israel's stance and will induce the Arabs to divulge their extremism
Criticism of Israeli policy	Too hawkish, main obstacle to peace	Wavering, not decisive enough in adopting a strong position	Policy has good intention but is ill-advised; does not know how to manage its inconsistencies; is squeamish in pointing out Arab extremism

nine

The Arab and Israeli Schools of Thought Compared

At this point it might be asked how the two sets of schools compare. In the study of conflicts the search for symmetries, mutual misconceptions, and mirror images has become commonplace. Such search may sometimes be a counsel of laziness, as it simplifies the task at hand of studying only one rival and then duplicating the findings, attributing them, without too much ado, to the other. For political scientists and psychologists this may serve as a means of manifesting their ability to rise above partisanship, of proving both neutrality and profundity by pointing out that both sides share in human frailties. True, there may be symmetries in conflicts; for instance, a harsh stance on one side may call forth greater harshness from the other, and probing for symmetries is perfectly legitimate. Nonetheless, it is more rewarding to search for asymmetries, which may then bring out the idiosyncrasies of each side and the fine differences which the search for symmetries may gloss over.

The Arab-Israeli conflict has been extremely asymmetrical in many of its aspects—the actors, their positions and sizes, their objectives, the stakes, and their ways of operation. To compare, for instance, the objective of politicide and the objective of annexation of the West Bank, to compare the Palestinians and the Israelis in their need for a homeland, or how uncompromising or intransigent their positions toward each other have been, may be fallacious.

That I have organized the thinking into *three* schools on both sides was neither deliberate for the sake of parallelism or symmetry nor motivated by aesthetic considerations; it is the outcome of my attempt to classify without any preconceived paradigm. True, a triad has merit in ordering: politically, left, center, and right; logically, as in an Aristotelian scheme, beginning, middle, and end. Actually, according to the logic of classification, there should have been on the Israeli side a fourth school—"dovish-hawkish" —yet this proved to be a null set.[1] Thus the classification of the schools was not guided by one principle of division, placing them in one continuum. Although the Israeli classification can be seen as following the political spectrum of left (first school), center (third school), and right (second school), such a classification does not apply to the Arab schools of thought.

Comparing the two sets of schools may throw some light on their mutual positions.

The Israeli "dovish-dovish" school has no parallel on the Arab side. No one of the Arab schools criticizes the Arab position on the basis of its justice or morality; each criticizes it only on its efficiency or on how realistic it is as to yielding the expected results.

The Israeli "hawkish-hawkish" school represents a vindictiveness that is shared by all three Arab schools. It is holist-totalistic in terms of demanding the whole of the occupied areas, in the manner of the Arab first and third schools demanding the demise of Israel in its entirety. This school, which is the most Zionist in its inspiration, is the most uncompromising in the nature of its demands and the most similar to the Arab schools, although here too there is a pronounced asymmetry, in that it does not aspire to deny either the Arabs or the Palestinians a political entity of their own; thus it is more relativist.

Both the third Israeli school and the second Arab school are reality-oriented. Both give importance to world public opinion. Both are flexible enough to encompass two open courses of action—tactics and strategy—yet on the conditions for activating each of these courses they diverge. The offer of concessions by the third Israeli school would shift from tactics to strategy according to *Arab responses*. On the Arab side, the expressed readiness to conclude a settlement with Israel would go from tactics (as a primary means of shrinking Israeli territory) to strategy (readiness to coexist and finalize the conflict) according to the *will or whim of the next Arab generation* or according to how propitious the political circumstances are for the continuation of the conflict and the achievement of the demise of Israel.

The second Israeli and third Arab schools share a cynical outlook on international relations. Both downgrade winning favorable public opinion as compared with the achievement of material assets.

The first Arab and second Israeli schools share an optimism about the historical trend, but they differ in the source and nature of their confidence. For the first Arab school the demise of Israel follows from its being by definition an anachronistic state. The second Israeli school, to the contrary, derives its confidence both from the self-exertion of the Israelis, who it holds will be ready for a greater effort to ensure the existence of their state than the Arab effort to destroy it, and from the inspiration of Jewish history. That is to say, this school assumes that since the Jews have survived many ordeals, they will survive this one too.

: *ten* :

Conclusion

The general approach of this work is open to the severe criticism of being *apolitical,* an abstraction from concrete reality, ignoring factors such as the super-powers and their interests, *détente,* the oil weapon, the Arab windfall of affluence and influence, the politics of the third world, tensions and dissensions in inter-Arab politics, the complications of the Lebanese war, etc. The whole political drama is reduced to an intellectual tug-of-war between such metaphysical entities as ethereal schools of thought, and to a forensic exercise. Not pallid philosophies, but interests and instincts are the blood and flesh of politics and history.

In response to the above criticism, I might say that the concrete factors of political reality have not been overlooked. They were included in my analysis as inputs in the contestants' evaluation of political reality. The behavior of nations is influenced not directly by the so-called facts of reality, but vicariously by images of these facts. To attempt to explain human behavior is to intellectualize it, by analyzing the conceptions in the actors' minds and the other motivations that have prompted their behavior. Thus what is required is a political and psychological explanation. Man is an ideological animal, and in order to understand his behavior there is need first to explore how he explains his behavior to himself, even if his explanation is only a rationalization, and then to evaluate it critically, taking into account other factors which man himself hesitates to acknowledge. The ideology of a political actor is the lens through which he sees reality. His ideology does not determine each of his decisions or acts, some of which may even be incompatible with it; nevertheless, his ideology gives a meaning, a direction, or an orientation to his general outlook and behavior. This work does not pretend to give an account of the day-to-day developments of the conflict, but only a summation of one important factor in it—how the rivals view the problems facing them in their confrontation with each other.

Such an approach may have the merit of dealing with essentials and with patterns of standing validity. In probing contemporary politics one is frequently tempted to consider periodic fluctuations as signifying irreversible new trends or to treat ripples as if they were waves. Thus a certain event or a political announcement is characterized as ushering in a new phase of great significance. Frequently it turns out afterwards to have been only a transient phenomenon, leaving no change in the basic patterns or basic positions of the political actors. To mention a few recent examples: Lessons were supposed to have been learned from Egypt's being isolated in the Arab world after the September 1975 interim agreement, and conclusions as to future developments were deduced from it; yet only a few months later Syria found itself the one that was isolated, owing to its armed intervention in Lebanon. The earlier alignment of the PLO with Syria against Egypt fell apart as the PLO and Syrian troops clashed in Lebanon in the summer of 1976, and the PLO became aligned with Egypt. The tension between Egypt and the Soviet Union was described as an irreparable rift, and this too may prove to be an exaggeration. The quarrel between Syria and Egypt proved to be temporary, as did their friendship. The Arabs have fought each other ferociously and the number of casualties in inter-Arab wars has been many times greater than casualties in the Arabs' wars and skirmishes with Israel, yet the Arab enmity toward Israel has not been tempered, whatever commentators may imply. Inter-Arab conflicts may diffuse some of the acuity in the Arab-Israeli confrontation, though so far they have signified only a pause in the conflict. Nor did the fact that the Syrian armed intervention in Lebanon was tolerated by Israel mean, as an American TV observer interpreted it, that relations between Syria and Israel had improved. Commentators frequently hailed certain declarations by PLO personalities as signifying a change in the PLO stand, and this too turned out to be premature. Thus many of the current events which seem at the time to be of great consequence turn out to be irrelevant in their influence on the basic confrontation between Israel and the Arabs. They may constitute a hindrance to understanding rather than a help. History, to be understood, has to be stripped of many dazzling events.

The mistake of exaggerating the importance of a particular event into a historical turning point is common, precisely because it is based on the human urge to search for the spectacular, the epoch-making event, and to take pride in having discerned it. To report "no change" is humdrum.

Contemporary history is not static, and important changes do intervene. Yet a true discrimination between its dynamic and static aspects, its continuity and discontinuity, is not easily achieved. Many seemingly important day-to-day events are soon consigned to oblivion. Many events that seem new turn out to be variations on the old, and some important real changes may pass unnoticed. Wisdom is the ability to view the close-up event in its true dimensions, as we would view it six months hence, without the magnifying and distorting effects that proximity produces. In the history of the Arab-Israeli conflict the mistake of evaluating certain events as heralding a new period and a change in the positions of the rivals has been common.

The advantage of the methodology followed in this essay is that it aims at bringing out "positions" which are not so volatile, but have a certain staying power. It is corrective to the tendency to see change because we wish and anticipate it. It describes the ideological ballast that has to be thrown overboard before a change can be achieved. The validity of such an approach will someday lapse, as changes which now seem unlikely may come true. We may hope that such a day is imminent and still maintain a skeptical, judicious view as to how near it may be. Such a cautionary attitude will fortify us to meet future events and developments.

There is another aspect deserving consideration. The factors of world politics—the politics of the big powers, oil, etc.—are indeed important. However, Israel can do very little about them. Israel cannot influence the relation between the United States and the Soviet Union. Israel cannot cause the disappearance of Arab oil. All these factors should be treated as data. The problem facing Israel is what to do about those factors within its power to manipulate.

The future is open. Any attempt to impose a straitjacket on developments, owing to some logical determinism or to an imperative deduced from a theory about the nature of conflict, would indeed be frivolous. Without claiming certainty, my guess about possible future developments is that the Arabs are not yet ready to really terminate the conflict, though they have made some progress toward it. Israeli concessions may thus prove to have only tactical value, and this only if world public opinion is appreciative of such offers.

Some American political commentators in important articles and pamphlets on the Arab-Israeli conflict in the last years have solicited Israel's withdrawal, yet stressed that it should take place only after a clear Arab commitment to finalize the conflict and even, according to some commentators, develop positive contents for peace such as diplomatic relations between the Arab states and Israel.[1] The test of the seriousness of these views would be the reaction of their authors if Arab leaders should reject such proposals, insisting on Israel's withdrawal, yet sticking to open-endedness about peace. The Arabs would brandish the words "peace," "political settlement," and "peaceful," but apply them to the *process* of Israel's withdrawal by peaceful means, not to the final destination to which the negotiations should lead. Israel will refuse to the best of its ability to withdraw in the face of such Arab maneuvers. Thus an impasse may ensue. In such a case a short-term policy of containing the conflict to keep it from escalating into war might be best policy.

Eventually the Western countries—and in particular the United States—might be driven to make a choice between tolerating Arab maneuvers, direct or indirect, to push Israel to its demise, or supporting Israel in preserving itself. The alternatives might rather narrow down. The effort of the first Arab school of thought is directed precisely at dealing with such an eventuality —to sugarcoat this dilemma, which the West will have to face, by producing the circumstances that would bring Israel to its demise seemingly without direct Arab effort. In face of such an effort Israel may have to assume a most resistant, obstinate or even a hawkish attitude, although dovishness should precede it so that Israel may accumulate political assets. Such developments might be protracted due to Arab involvement in inter-Arab quarrels, which would produce some kind of respite or pause on the front with Israel.

For Israel the conflict with its neighbors has become the major and central feature in its national life. The conflict ambience is not confined to its external policies, as the solution of its internal problems can be helped by mobilizing the readiness for sacrifice that the exigencies of the conflict produce. Despite its negative aspects, the conflict can become a great motivational force for greater national effort, internally and externally, and a powerful stimulus for excellence. People who, like the Israelis, find themselves facing such odds and adversities should be imbued with the conviction of the need to tax their ability to the maximum, including exerting themselves to improve the quality of life so as to make all the sacrifices worthwhile.

People are ready for hardships when they have hope that their suffering will end someday, to be succeeded by better times, or when they see light at the end of the tunnel. It is difficult to say how this conflict will end. Facile promises have too frequently been disproved, so one should be wary of producing happy scenarios. Israelis have been too disenchanted to go on giving credence to them. (This is the weakness of the first Israeli school.) Israelis need great sophistication, and understanding of the historical relativity of conflicts and their solutions. Most conflicts have not been solved by going through the movements of an exercise prescribed for their solution, but rather have petered out. They were not settled; they vanished. They had terminations rather than solutions. The natural urge to see the end, its details and its time, is understandable. But it should be balanced by the cultivation of some tolerance for uncertainty. The Arab-Israeli conflict is not unique in its resistance to solution; the world is full of issues the solutions to which are uncertain and not in sight. Pride in the ability to withstand the conflict and its ordeals can be a source of great popular satisfaction, compensating for the lack of clarity as to the details of its solution. The present crisis in Israel stems not from impatience while awaiting the solution of the conflict, but rather from a feeling of discontent and inadequacy about the way Israeli society meets its challenges.

The conflict may be protracted. This means that Israel should neither fatalistically resign itself to its continuation nor indulge in the rosy illusion that the end is imminent. Israelis should have the conviction that their government is doing its best to bring the conflict to an end, and that if it continues it is through no fault of Israel's. A conciliatory attitude toward the rival will give Israel the moral strength to withstand the ordeals of the conflict.

The Palestinian issue no doubt is central in this conflict. The Palestinians are a competent, active group. Their predicament has driven them to seek advancement by education. The number of their university graduates and academics is disproportionately high. They are more influential in the Arab world than their number warrants. In their literature they boast of being the flower of Arab societies.[2] Nevertheless, it remains to be seen whether they will become emissaries of chaos and destruction or of development and modernization. They may view themselves as both—destroyers of the old structures and builders of the new. However, through their ambition to subvert both Israel and Jordan and their inability to do so by themselves, they have tried to embroil other Arab societies in their struggle. This may lead to their becoming a nuisance to the other Arabs. Their pretensions to dictate the Arab line in the conflict, by virtue of their close knowledge of it or their direct involvement in it, have already produced a considerable amount of acrimony against them. Many Palestinians have been displaced in various Arab states, not only because these states prefer to give jobs previously held by Palestinians to their indigenous intelligentsia, but because of the Palestinians' reputation for subversion. The demands they make on Arab governments, arrogating to themselves roles these governments are unwilling to let them have, tend to put them on a collision course with these governments. This has already led to open conflict in Jordan, in September 1970, and with Syria in Lebanon in the summer of 1976, in both cases with tragic results for the Palestinians.

In desperation the Palestinians may develop apocalyptic, cataclysmic tendencies—such as Dr. Habash's declared wish for a third world war inasmuch as the Palestinians have nothing to lose from a global catastrophe. Their reverses in Lebanon may strengthen such trends at least in some Palestinian circles. But the Arab states do have a lot to lose, and may well see it differently, refusing to condemn themselves to endless upheavals simply because some Palestinians cannot find a solution that satisfies them. There is growing weariness of this conflict in Arab societies and consequently an urge to bring it to some end or at least to a more protracted pause. It seems to me (although I am loath to sermonize on what others' policy should be) that the Palestinians will have to lower their demands and work out a solution with Jordan.

Israel, too, has to set forth practical national objectives. This may require some rethinking on Zionism itself or in any case some changes in emphasis. Israel has hitherto benefited from Arab extremism, and the third school of Israeli thought seeks to continue exploiting such benefits. But such opportunities are not

Conclusion

likely to go on forever. The West Bank will remain Arab by virtue of its preponderant Arab population. Israel may not be able to transcend its destiny of remaining a small country. Yet the quality of life and the size of a country are not necessarily in direct correlation. It is the quality of life within the country that should be the real national objective, for it is this alone that will enable the people to withstand a prolonged conflict and to look to a healthy collective life beyond its termination.

Notes

Chapter One

1. Nasser summed it up in a speech in Alexandria on December 13, 1953, in criticizing Arab declarations which were not followed by action. "We used to say in our meetings and speeches we would throw the Jews into the sea. . . ." In *Speeches and Declarations of President Gamal abd al- Nasser, 1952–1959*, Ikhtarna Laka Edition, Vol. 1, Cairo, no date, page 154. Expressions of deep hostility against Israel and the Israelis and the vehement use of a host of verbal nouns, such as liquidation, wiping-out, cleansing, issuing a death verdict, smashing, destroying, eliminating, eradicating, etc., all give the impression that they were not meant metaphorically.

2. I have compiled a glossary of such expressions in Chap-

ter 1 of my book *Arab Attitudes to Israel,* Israel Universities Press, Jerusalem, Hart Publishing Co., New York; Vallentine Mitchell, London, 1972, 1976 in which the subject of verbal expressions of the Arab objective is analyzed in greater detail.

3. The concept of all-out war as well as the whole politicidal nexus could be linked to *Jihād,* the holy war by which Islam aspires to bring the entire world into its fold. Without denying their importance I prefer not to evoke Islamic archetypes and limit myself to a political analysis (which includes some psychology) without delving into the cultural aspects of this conflict.

   Nasser may have clung to the idea of an all-out war for psychological reasons beside the intellectual ones. The war in 1948, which ended in a completely unexpected defeat, was a major trauma for Nasser's generation. War (or, as it was then called, "a second round") may have seemed necessary to settle the account. Israel was established by war and by war it will be destroyed.

4. The UN General Assembly voted that the Mandatory territory of Palestine would be divided into two independent states—Arab and Jewish, linked by an economic union, with Jerusalem internationalized. The Arabs opposed this resolution violently, and Arab armies invaded the country as the British relinquished their rule. War ensued. Armistice agreements were concluded in 1949 separately between Egypt, Lebanon, Jordan, and Syria on the one hand and Israel on the other, at the behest of the Security Council. The agreements were based on the fighting lines which were more favorable to Israel than the boundaries of the Par-

tition resolution. They remained in force until the Six-Day War in 1967.

5. Arab indoctrination literature is of great interest. True, inward propaganda can be demagoguery and still be an important indicator of what the leaders want their public to believe. If its ideas are manipulated by the leaders in order to acquire popularity, they testify to what ideas are popular, for only by manipulating popular ideas can one acquire popularity. Arab indoctrination literature for their troops is of great value to understand official positions. See *The Palestinian Problem, a lecture by Mr. Sabri al-Khūlī, the personal representative of the President* (in Arabic), Supreme Command of Armed Forces (UAR—Egypt), Directorate of General Affairs and Spiritual Guidance [indoctrination, Y.H.], no date, probably 1966. (The author now serves as the Arab League mediator in Lebanon.) It is a blatantly anti-Israeli and anti-Semitic booklet.

6. *Fedayeen* is presently a name for Arab or Palestinian irregulars. Etymologically it comes from "sacrifice," i.e., those ready to sacrifice themselves. Historically this name was given in the twelfth century to those sent to assassinate the enemies of a Shiite sect popularly called "the assassins." Its meaning became diffused as a name for Arabs engaged in guerrilla warfare.

7. For details on the development of this thinking, see my *Fedayeen Action and Arab Strategy*, Adelphi Paper No. 53, The International Institute for Strategic Studies, London, December 1968.

8. Included in my book *Palestinians and Israel*, Keter Publishing House, Jerusalem; John Wiley & Sons, N.Y., 1974, p. 108.

9. Ahmad Shukairy is the founder of the Palestine Liberation Organization (PLO) and was its central leader
from 1964–1967.

During 1949–1964 the Palestinians did not have a
centrally recognized organization. In May 1964 such an
organization was established by a Palestinian Constituent Congress called by Ahmad Shukairy. Shukairy
acted by virtue of his earlier nomination by the Arab
League to the post of "representative of Palestine" in
the League and on the authority of a Summit meeting
of Arab rulers. The Constituent Congress became the
first in a series of National Councils which are the high-
est authority in the PLO deciding on its policy and programs. They convene periodically. The last one—the
twelfth—convened in June 1974.

The delegates of the Councils (numbering 100–400)
theoretically have to be elected by direct ballot by the
Palestinians, who are all considered "natural members"
of the PLO. However, there has never been such an
election and the delegates are nominated by a process
of bargaining between the organizations (mainly
Fedayeen) of which the PLO is composed. The Councils in their turn elect the "Executive Committee"
which directs the daily activities of the PLO. The
Chairman of the Executive Committee (presently Yasir
Arafat) is the head of the whole movement.

The central document setting the PLO platform is
the National Covenant or National Charter. The Covenant was first promulgated at the first Council in 1964
and amended at the fourth Council in April 1968. Since
then no amendments have been introduced into its text.

Notes

Chapter Two

1. Examples of the use of such language are found repeatedly in many pages in my book *Arab Attitudes to Israel*.

2. The Security Council Resolution 242 is presently the basic document for any negotiations on the conflict. It was promulgated on November 22, 1967 after long deliberations on the situation that transpired after the Six-Day War. It includes the following elements: inadmissibility of conquests, need to establish a just and lasting peace, withdrawal of Israeli troops from territories (not from "the" territories, i.e., not necessarily all of them) occupied in 1967, termination of belligerency, acknowledgment of sovereignty, territorial integrity and political independence of all states in the area and their right to live in peace within secure and recognized boundaries free from threats of acts of force, freedom of navigation, just settlement of the refugee problem, and the establishment of demilitarized zones.

Chapter Three

1. During Nasser's time in the period 1967–1973, this demand was sloganized as "wiping out the traces of aggression," which usually was left vague. When "1967 aggression" was specified, it meant withdrawal to the previous line, whereas specifying "1948 aggression" meant wiping out Israel, which allegedly was established by an act of aggression in 1948. The same

objective was expressed in PLO language as "wiping out the source of aggression" or "wiping out the instrument of aggression."

2. Significantly, the adoption of the slogan "democratic state" by the Eighth Council in February–March 1971 has not induced the amendment of the Palestinian National Covenant in its 1968 version, which contradicts it, despite the fact that there has been ample opportunity. Eight years have passed, and nine National Councils have been convened in the meantime. This is not simple oversight. There has been dogged opposition within the PLO to enshrining the slogan "democratic state" in the National Covenant, as such a step would give the slogan the stature of a national tenet, whereas the opposing circles consider it merely a tactical phrase. This casts grave doubts on the Palestinian appearance of moderation. The slogan itself has been grossly misunderstood outside the Arab world. It does not at all mean binationality, but rather that the Palestinian state is designed to be *Arab*, merged within an *Arab unity*, with a minority of Jews who have shed their Israeli, i.e., Zionist, character.

This contradiction between the Covenant and the slogan has been remarked by Palestinians. Thus Sabri Jiryis of the PLO Research Center in Beirut in a programmatic article stated:

First of all, a few amendments should be introduced in the Palestinian National Covenant, on the one hand, and an end should be put to some 'undemocratic' manifestations in the behavior of those supporting the democratic state on the other. To begin with the famous Article 6 ("The

Jews who had normally resided in Palestine until
the beginning of the Zionist invasion will be
considered Palestinian") should be abrogated or
amended. The only meaning this article has is
that 99 percent of the Jews living today in Palestine should be evicted from their abodes. This
causes great damage to the Palestinians in various progressive circles in the world. There is
neither need, nor logic, to leave this article in its
present form, which testifies to an exaggerated
aggravation as compared with the previous article in the original Covenant (Article 7 in the
1964 version of the Covenant). And this while
the Palestinian National Council confirms in all
its sessions since 1969 till this day, by a decisive
vote, the slogan 'democratic state,' and while
Arafat as Chairman of the Executive Committee
of the Palestine Liberation Organization and the
Commander-in-Chief of the Palestinian Revolution declares to the representatives of the world
in the UN that 'when we speak of our common
hopes for the Palestine of tomorrow we include
in our perspective all Jews now living in Palestine who choose to live with us there in peace and
without discrimination.' Other articles which are
of the same thrust of meaning as this article
should also be amended. *Al-Nahār*, Beirut, May
15, 1975, p. 10.
3. *Newsweek*, January 5, 1976, p. 30.
4. All the Palestinian National Councils, from July 4,
1968, to January 11, 1973, included strong resolutions
against such a state. The Twelfth (June 1974) agreed

to a "Palestinian authority" on the condition that it not entail a political settlement.

5. Official report, *PLO, the Palestinian Popular Congress and Tenth Extraordinary Council*, April 6–12, 1972, p. 105. "Entire homeland" refers to all the territory of Palestine; see Palestinian National Covenant (in Arabic), Articles 1–2.

6. The theme that Palestine and Israel are mutually exclusive is prominent in PLO writings, and the conflict is frequently presented as a deadly zero-sum game. "We say 'no' to Israel because we say 'yes' to Palestine," Professor Fayez Sayegh, quoted by Ibrahim al-'Abd, *A Handbook to Palestine Questions* (2d ed.), PLO Research Center, Beirut, 1971, p. 174. Saying "yes" to both Palestine and Israel is excluded. Professor Sayegh is a Palestinian who has written extensively on the Arab-Israeli conflict, has taught at the American University of Beirut, and is presently Counselor to the Kuwaiti Government.

7. See Palestinian National Covenant, Article 20.

8. For a thorough analysis of the democratic state's anti-dream programmatic features, see the article by Dr. Mahjub 'Omar, "Democratic Palestine, a Trend, a Programme and an Historic Imperative," in *Shu'un Filastiniyya*, January–February 1975.

9. It is worth noting that both UN resolutions were rejected by the then Arab UN member-states. The USSR, the Ukraine, Byelorussia, and Czechoslovakia voted with the Arab states against the resolution of December 11, 1948.

10. The Palestinians, i.e., people entitled to live in the Palestinian state, are, according to Article 5 of the

Palestinian National Covenant, all *Arabs* born to a Palestinian father, without regard to their present nationality. This definition constitutes a Palestinian "Law of Return." Palestinians may have double nationality, whereas in the case of the Jews double nationality is condemned.

Since the returning Palestinians will demand former land property in Israel, there will arise a clash between their rights to it and those of the Jews now living on such property in places like Ramle, Beersheba, Lod, Jerusalem, etc. The Political Committee in its report to the Palestinian Congress and the Tenth Council referred to such an eventuality, taking the position that the government of Liberated Palestine will side with those who supported the "Palestinian Revolution," i.e., the Arabs. What follows from such a stand is that many Jews will have to evacuate their abodes. This indirectly was referred to in Arafat's speech in the UN, and in other Palestinian declarations that the Jews will be accepted in Liberated Palestine on condition that they do not claim to enjoy "discrimination," that their demands should not have precedence over Arab demands; this means that in practice Jews will have to yield.

11. From the rules of prudence in situations of conflict which I formulated in a booklet published for the Israeli troops by the Armed Forces Chief Education Officer in November 1967, included in my book *Palestinians and Israel*, Keter Publishing House, Jerusalem, and John Wiley & Sons, N.Y. and Toronto, 1974, p. 191.

A relativist approach is the extension of the Kantian categorical imperative to the international sphere. In it, pragmatic considerations of avoiding overstepping for fear of provoking a backlash converge with moral considerations of recognizing the adversary's full stature. A relativist approach means searching for common interests with the adversary as means to achieve conciliation. An absolutist approach causes the primitivization of a conflict reducing it to a deadly quarrel of survival and a zero-sum game.

12. *Palestine Lives, Interviews with Leaders of the Resistance,* Palestine Research Center and Kuwaiti Teachers Association, 1973, p. 162 (italics in the original).

Chapter Four

1. This school's viewpoint is expressed succinctly by Haytham al-Ayubi's article "Future Arab Strategy in the Light of the Fourth War," in *Shu'un Filastiniyya,* October 1974. An English translation of the article with my annotations was published by the Israel Universities Study Group for Middle Eastern Affairs, Jerusalem. Isma'il Sabri Abdulla's book *Confronting Israel,* Cairo, 1969, can be considered as a guide to both the first and the second schools of thought, as it has elements of both. Sabri Abdulla served as Egyptian Minister of Planning in 1972 and 1973.

2. Elias Murqus, *The Palestinian Resistance and the Present Situation,* Dār al-Haqīqa, Beirut, April 1971, p. 81.

3. The Arab term for this, which Al-Ayubi uses, is

dhubūl. A similar idea inheres in the term "shrinking," *inkimāsh* in Arabic. Lutfī al-Khūlī concludes his article "One October and a New Style" thus: "Any peaceful solution means the contraction of Israel. Israel is deeply convinced that an contraction means the beginning of the end for the Zionist entity." *Al-Nahār*, December 18, 1975. The expression "withering away" is most probably borrowed from Marxist theory about the withering away of states when socialism is established and the state is no longer needed as an instrument for class oppression. Here, the withering away process is not universal, but focused on a single state.

4. The debate on Bourguiba's proposals is most instructive for understanding the problematics of Arab attitudes and the difficulties they grapple with. A brilliant articulation of the criticism of the gradualist approach is found in Professor Fayez Sayegh's booklet *A Handful of Fog: A Study in the Conceptual Structure of Bourghibism and Its Slogan* (in Arabic), PLO Research Center, Beirut, July 1966.

What Bourguiba meant in his proposals was subject to a dispute in Israel. Fādil Jamālī (Iraq's former Minister for Foreign Affairs and Professor of Education at the University of Tunis) can be relied on to give a correct description: "There is a conception calling for following the policy of "take and demand more" [terms Bourguiba used to characterize his proposal and his philosophy of life (Y.H.)] or "the policy of phases" in order to benefit from the international circumstances, so that in the meantime the Arabs prepare themselves militarily and thus restore their rights completely without any deficiency." Fādil Jamālī, *Memories and Lessons*, second edition, Dār al-Kitāb al-Jadīd, Beirut, 1965, p. 10. Thus the final aim was the demise of Israel.

5. Sadat can be considered the spokesman for this school. He has expressed his views in many speeches and press interviews. See, too, Lutfī al-Khūlī's series of articles, "Sadat's Political Doctrine," in *Al-Ahrām* and *Al-Nahār* during June–September 1975.

6. The readiness to recognize Israel as a fact is, no doubt, an important political step. However, in itself it cannot serve as proof of Arab reconciliation to Israel, as some commentators argue. Recognition of the existence of an object is implied in all designs to undo it.

7. When such a group becomes weightier in terms of membership and political influence, we shall have to set up a fourth school—of peace *as termination* of the conflict. It will be a great day for all sides.

In previous brief treatments of the typology of Arab views (in *Gesher*, No. 72–73, December 1972, and a paper submitted in May 1973 to a conference at the Van Leer Institute in Jerusalem) I anticipated such a fourth school, though I qualified it in the paper:

What is the political importance of the *public circles* in Egypt that advocate peace as the termination of the conflict? We know about their existence partly from occasional sentences in which they express themselves, but most of our information is derived indirectly, from criticism leveled against them by the press; this criticism reflects the rejection of their stand by the government.

These voices, it should be stressed, have not reached the state of the Samizdat (underground literature) found in the Soviet Union. As the United States cannot base its policy toward the Soviet Union on the Samizdat and must relate to the position of the decision-making elite, so Israel cannot base its policy on these faint dissident voices. If we deal with this phenomenon in a political and not in a folklorist fashion, its importance, for the time being, is marginal. These circles will be important when they are influential within the Egyptian government. (Included in my *Palestinians and Israel*, Keter Publishing House, Jerusalem, 1974, p. 200.)

Apparently these intellectuals were impressed afterwards by the Egyptian achievement in October 1973 and acknowledged their support of Sadat's policy. They thus forfeited their particularity and joined the second school. There is a possibility that now, as they realize that peace has not arrived, they, or at least Mahfūz, are ready to go further and make a concession in territory to meet Israel's sensitivity to security. It would be a remarkable change, which perhaps limits even further the number of people who would support it.

8. The demand that Israel should shrink further than the 1967 borders is repeatedly aired by Egyptian spokesmen. Isma'il Fahami, Egyptian Minister for Foreign Affairs, stressed this in an interview with the Viennese *Couriere* of June 7, 1975, when he was asked whether "the area of the Jewish state need not necessarily be

identified with that before June 1967." He retorted, "It should be smaller." "Smaller?" "Certainly."

9. *Shu'un Filastiniyya*, No. 14, October 1972, p. 224.

10. Resolution 338 was adopted by the UN Security Council on October 22, 1973. It called for a cease-fire and to start immediately the implementation of Resolution 242.

11. *Shu'un Filastiniyya*, No. 14, October 1972, p. 18.

12. Dār Al-Qadāyā, Beirut, 1975.

13. *At-Tali'a*, September 1975, p. 15.

14. *Ibid.*

15. *Ibid.*, pp. 16–17.

16. A lucid summary of the arguments of this school is presented in an article by Professor Fayez Sayegh, "Comments on the Security Council Resolution 242," in *Shu'un Filastiniyya*, November 1972.

17. This conference, convened in September 1967 to coordinate Arab policy after the Six-Day War, decided: ". . . to ensure the withdrawal of Israeli forces from the Arab territories occupied during the June War, provided that it be consistent with the principles to which all Arab nations adhere: that there shall be no peace with Israel, no recognition of Israel, no negotiations with Israel." F. A. Jaber, *International Documents on Palestine 1967*, The Institute for Palestine Studies, Beirut, 1970, p. 657.

18. Sadat calls the Arab world "the sixth super power" (quoted by Cairo Radio, September 8, 1975, from Sadat's interview with *As-Siāsah*).

19. An expression of this combination may be found, for example, in a remark by President Ja'afar Numeiri of

Sudan, who said in an interview with *Al-Anwār* on February 13, 1975: "Wiping Israel off the face of the earth is an impossible task. Israel will devour itself, and we must leave this to history."

20. The Rejection Front is composed of several Fedayeen organizations, the most important of which is the Popular Front for the Liberation of Palestine headed by Dr. George Habash. (Second in importance is the Arab Liberation Front organized by Iraq.) The Rejection Front opposes adamantly any political settlement of the conflict and in particular participation in a Geneva Conference. To emphasize its stand, Habash's Popular Front withdrew in September 1974 from its membership in the PLO Executive Committee, but it retains its membership in the Palestinian National Council.

21. Ba'ath (Resurrection) Party was established in Syria in the early forties. It vehemently advocated the idea of Arab Unity. Since March 1963 it is the ruling party in Syria. Iraq came under the Ba'ath party in July 1968. Though both parties call themselves Ba'athist and draw inspiration from its doctrines, they have a sharp quarrel on political and ideological issues aggravated by their being splits of what used to be one party.

22. The Twelfth National Congress of the Ba'ath party (Syria) in July 1975 adopted the policy termed in the resolution "Strategy of Phases," stipulating that the final objective is the dismantlement of Israel which will be achieved in a step-by-step fashion. In this resolution territorial interim agreements (involving Israel's withdrawals) are accepted, provided they do not im-

pair the possibility of continuing the struggle against Israel.

Chapter Six

1. Demonstration was partially a matter of retaliatory actions against Arab marauding. The launching of such raids was a thorny problem. First, there were adverse results in world public opinion; second, such actions were not always completely controlled, and in many cases a degree of military success which was not foreseen or intended caused political embarrassment; third, they required a delicate sense of measurement—neither to underreact, which might incite the Arabs to more audacious provocations and greater confidence in their strength, nor to overreact, which would only result in greater effort to build their forces, out of frustration and a thirst for revenge. Israel, as a young nation in the making and irked by stubborn Arab rejection of it, tended to overreact. Often retaliatory action was initiated simply out of bewilderment, out of not knowing how to react, since doing nothing at all was insufferable.

2. Demonstrating empathy toward the Arab grievance against Zionism and calling for an "ideological disarmament" on both sides was a main theme in my booklet *Israel's Position in Its Conflict with the Arabs* (in Hebrew), Dvir, Tel Aviv, 1967. In a shorter French version, the essay was included in *Temps modernes,* Vol. 293, dedicated to the Arab-Israeli conflict, Paris, 1967. (The essay was written almost two years before the Six-Day War.) A full Arabic translation was published in 1968 in Tel Aviv by the Histadrut publishing house.

Its distribution was limited, as books published in Israel are not allowed in Arab countries, and the reaction to it was at most inconclusive.

3. From a paper submitted to the Seventh Annual Conference of the London Institute for Strategic Studies, October 1965. The word "politicide" was used for the first time in this paper.

4. I have analyzed these aspects and their detailed manifestations in my book *Arab Attitudes to Israel*, Israel Universities Press, Jerusalem, 1972, 1976, Hart Publishing Co., New York, 1972; Vallentine Mitchell, London 1972; Chapter 4.

5. The refusal of the Israeli Foreign Office in 1970 to use and distribute the 1968 Palestinian National Covenant, which I annotated, epitomizes the whole approach. I was very bluntly told that its publication in English, in order to bring the PLO position to the attention of public opinion, would be against Israel's interests. Afterwards this policy changed, culminating in January 1976 in the distribution of the Covenant with my annotations as a UN document to all UN members on the initiative of the Israeli representative. The previous lack of understanding of how this document could be of great use for the Israeli case has all these years intrigued and deeply worried me, as a symptom of Israel's failure to understand its own situation.

6. An example of such treatment is a statement by Deputy Assistant Secretary of State Harold H. Saunders in the US Congress, November 12, 1975. Saunders described the PLO objective as if it might mean "a binational secular state," which is not correct, as the PLO calls its state *Arab*, though a Jewish minority would be allowed

to live in it. This minority would be Jewish in religion but Arab in its nationality. No wonder that the official organ of the PLO criticized harshly the Saunders statement (*Filastin Ath-Thavra*, November 30, 1975, p. 5).

Chapter Seven

1. The PLO's attitudes toward Jordan and Israel are not symmetrical. It aspires to destroy Israel's *infrastructure* and Jordan's *superstructure;* to change the *state* in the first case, to change the *regime* in the second.
2. Such as *Filastinistan* (association with Arabistan as an Arab region in Iranian bondage), *Duweila* (ministate derogatorily), and *Al-Kian al-Hazil* (the emaciated entity).
3. Arab spokesmen in the press and in radio interviews, when asked to explain the causes of the Lebanese internal war, too frequently have resorted to placing all blame on Israel and the US. Thus there are no internal problems in Lebanon, only external machinations. A nonguilt complex can be no less harmful than an excessive guilt complex, as it makes self-improvement superfluous.
4. Anne R. Zahlan (ed.), *International Documents on Palestine 1971*, Institute for Palestine Studies, Beirut, and the University of Kuwait, 1974, p. 398.
5. *Ibid.* This resolution repeated an earlier formulation contained in an agreement to which all the Fedayeen groups acceded for the first time, signifying a landmark in the history of the PLO. This document is called: "Statement by the Unified Command of the Palestinian

Resistance Movement Declaring a Formula for National Unity and a Program for Political and Military Action" (Amman, May 6, 1970). It stated in article 2: "The Palestinian struggle is based on the belief that the people in the Palestinian-Jordanian theatre are one people, that the people of Palestine are part of the Arab nation and that the territory of Palestine is part of Arab territory." Walid Khadduri (ed.), *International Documents on Palestine 1970*, The Institute of Palestine Studies, Beirut, and the University of Kuwait, 1973, p. 795.

6. An article setting forth the necessity of subverting Jordan calls Jordan the "Palestine of East Jordan"; the West Bank is termed "Central Palestine," while the whole area including Israel is termed "Greater Palestine." 'Isām Sakhninī in *Shu'un Filastiniyya*, September 1975, pp. 22–26.

7. According to the 1954 Jordanian Nationality Law (article 2), anyone residing in Jordan who used to have the Palestinian nationality, excluding Jews, is regarded as a Jordanian citizen. On February 4, 1960 the Jordanian government decided to grant Jordanian citizenship to all Palestinians living abroad who wished to acquire it.

8. Massacre of the Assyrians in Iraq in 1933; long war against the Kurds until March 1975 and subsequent persecutions; Yemenite civil war from 1962–1967, in which Egypt intervened; suppression of Fedayeen organizations in 1970–1971 in which the Palestinians claim they had thousands of casualties; suppression of the revolt of the South Sudanese which caused casualties and refugees numbering hundreds of thousands. The number of dead in the current civil war in Lebanon is claimed to surpass forty thousand. The fre-

quency of cases of mutilation of the dead in Arab kill-
ings is ominous.

Chapter Eight

1. An example is the slogan "Peace or settlements." The
   policy of setting up settlements in the occupied areas is
   perhaps ill-advised, as these settlements would not
   change the population coloring of these areas, and the
   policy only gives the Arabs a propaganda pretext. However, it is wrong to argue, as implied in this slogan,
   that had there been no such settlements there would
   have been peace, or that these settlements are the main
   obstacle to peace.

   The sheer incessant harping by spokesmen of this
   school on the notion of peace, their incessant caressing
   it, can be psychologically gratifying for them as proof
   of their sublime idealism. However, their peace plans
   by implication credit the Arab position with being not
   completely averse to peace as they envision it.

2. Significantly the UN General Assembly Partition Resolution of November 29, 1947 (Resolution 181 II) refers
   to the establishment side by side of a "Jewish state"
   and an "*Arab* state," not a Palestinian state. No Arab or
   Palestinian protested. The resolution used the term
   "Palestinian citizens" as applying to all Arabs, Jews
   and others who had naturalized in Mandate Palestine.

3. The argument that a Palestinian state may become a
   Soviet base is practically valid, still it is doubtful as a
   matter of principle. Other neighboring states, too, may
   become Soviet bases, but that does not warrant their
   occupation by Israel. Furthermore, it brings up the

whole problem of the right of intervention to influence a foreign country's regime.

4. Brith-Shalom and Ihud were small groups during the British Mandate who were most conciliatory toward the Arabs to the point of readiness to forgo the core value of the Zionist ideology—Jewish statehood—and settle for binationalism, namely, an Arab-Jewish state.

   The Revisionist movement was the nationalist wing in Zionism and precursor of the present Herut party.

5. I made this suggestion in an earlier newspaper article, "Reflections on Israel's Policy in the Conflict," *Ma'ariv* (in Hebrew), May 10, 1970, and is included in my book *Palestinians and Israel*, Keter Publishing House, Jerusalem, and John Wiley & Sons, New York and Toronto; 1974, p. 181.

6. Spokesmen of the first Israeli school unwittingly pretend to present the Arab or Palestinian position more faithfully than the Palestinians and Arabs themselves. The Israeli daily *Al-Hamishmar* on September 6, 1976 quoted one of the prominent members of this school reproaching the Palestinians: "The Jewish public hears about Palestinian preparedness to live in peace with Israel only from our mouths, not from Palestinian spokesmen." Apparently he claims clairvoyance.

Chapter Nine

1. The Israeli schools of thought in a fourfold matrix:

		ISRAEL'S RESPONSES	
		Dovish	*Hawkish*
CONCEPTIONS OF	*Dovish*	School I	null set, or empty cell
ARAB POSITION OR STRATEGY	*Hawkish*	School III	School II

Notes

Chapter Ten

1. See, for instance, "Toward Peace in the Middle East," the Brookings Institution, Washington, 1975.
2. Anis al-Qasim, in discussing the effect of the Palestinian dispersion in the Arab world: "History will acknowledge that the Palestinians have carried the Arab world from the Middle Ages into the Twentieth Century. They have skillfully played a major role in the development of the Arab world." *From the Wilderness of Jerusalem* (in Arabic), Tripoli, Libya, 1965, p. 21. Muhammed Abu Shilbaya: "This people [the Palestinians] is the salt of these countries [the Arab] and has provided them with what is good, grasping their hands in order to lift them from the frozen shadows of backwardness to light, the light of culture and progress in science, in knowledge and in toil, in schools, in universities, the press, factories, and the green fields that have been created from yellow arid wilderness." *The Road to Redemption, Liberation and Peace* (in Arabic), Jerusalem, no date, p. 13.

Index

After the Guns Fall Silent (Sid-Ahmad), 57

Algeria
"continuous strife" school and, 76
guerrilla warfare, 13, 14

Alsace-Lorraine, 43

Anti-Semitism, 91, 93

Anwār, Al-, 55

Arab League, 12

Arab policy, 3–77; *see also* Israeli policy
"continuous strife" school, 19, 63–78, 156
"erosion and withering away" school, 19, 41–46, 53, 62–63, 70–77, 123, 156, 162–163
in fifties and sixties, 3–16
guerrilla warfare, 13–16, 21, 42, 64
incrementalism, 13, 19–22, 24, 65, 72
Israel's withdrawal, 27–28, 42–43, 45, 48, 50, 64

Nasser and, 8–12, 19–22, 62, 68
Palestinian problem: *see* Palestinian problem
"phases method," 45–46
"reducing Israel to its natural dimensions" school, 19, 47–63, 66, 70–77, 123, 155
schools of thought compared to Israel's, 153–156
war *à outrance,* 8–12

Arafat, Yasir, 32–33, 36, 120

Asad, Hafez al-, 103

Awad, Louis, 51

Ba'ath ideology, 77, 103

Borchgrave, Arnaud de, 58, 59

Bourguiba, Habib, 10, 45, 46

Brest-Litovsk, Treaty of, 43

Brith-Shalom movement, 141

British Mandate period (1917–1948), 5

Capital punishment, 121

China, guerrilla warfare in, 13
Communist parties (Arab), 76
"Continuous strife" school, 19,
    63–77, 156
  schematic typology of, 74–75
Covenant of the Palestine Liber-
    ation Organization, 35–36,
    108, 113, 114
Cuba, guerrilla warfare in, 13

Détente, 20–21, 57–58, 132
"Dovish-dovish" school, 128–
    133, 139, 140, 142–143, 148,
    150–152, 154–155, 164
  differences between other
    schools and, 150–151

Egypt, 28, 121
  October 1973 war, 48
  PLO and, 159
  "reducing Israel to its natural
    dimensions" school and, 47–
    52, 54–63, 100–101, 103
  Syria and, 159
  U.S.S.R. and, 159
Eighth Palestinian National
    Council (1971), 118–119
"Erosion and withering away"
    school, 19, 41–46, 53, 62–63,
    70–77, 123, 156, 162–163
  schematic typology of, 74–75

Fatah, al, 21, 76
Fedayeen, 13–16, 17, 21, 74

Gaza strip, 28, 30, 31, 49, 115,
    117, 131
General Assembly of December
    11, 1948, 33
Ghali, Boutros de, 58, 61
Golan Heights, 133
Guerrilla warfare, 13–16, 21, 42,
    64

Habash, George, 166

Hawādeth, Al-, 57
Haifa, 134
Hakīm, Tufīq al-, 51
"Hawkish-dovish" school, 134,
    140–151, 155
  differences between other
    schools and, 150–151
"Hawkish-hawkish" school, 133–
    140, 142–144, 150–151, 155,
    156
  differences between other
    schools and, 150–151
Hebron, 134
Heikal, Muhammad Hassanein,
    63
Historical determinism, 72
"Historical rights," claim of, 134
Hussein, King of Jordan, 116,
    119

Ihud movement, 141
Incrementalism, 13, 19–22, 24,
    65, 72
Indoctrination, 13
Iraq, 77, 121
  "continuous strife" school, 76
Islam, 61
Israeli policy, 81–151; *see also*
    Arab policy
  after 1973, 100–109
  concessions, need for, 111–122
  "dovish-dovish" school, 128–
    133, 139, 140, 142–143, 148,
    150–151, 154–155, 164
  evolution of, 85–109
  "hawkish-dovish" school, 134,
    140–151, 155
  "hawkish-hawkish" school, 133–
    140, 142–144, 150–151, 155,
    156
  1949–1967, 90–94, 96
  1967–1973, 94–100
  objections to concessions policy,
    122–125

Index

Palestinian problem: *see* Palestinian problem
schools of thought compared to Arab, 153–156
Six-Day War, 94–96
withdrawal question, 103–105, 111–112, 125, 128, 133, 142, 162
world public opinion and, 87–91

Jaish ash-Sha'ab, 66
Jordan, 16, 28, 31, 67, 73, 97, 115–121, 131, 166

Kaddoumi, Farouk, 29, 30
Khartum Arab summit conference, 67
Khūlī, Luftī al-, 58
Kissinger, Henry, 106
Knesset, 93

League of Nations, 35
Lebanon, 16, 124, 136
Syrian intervention, 159, 166
Lenin, V. I., 43
Libya, 76
Lod airport, 133

Mahfūz, Nagīb, 51
Mandate of the League of Nations, 35
Mandate period (1917–1948), 5
Mao Tse-tung, 14
Mūhi ad-Dīn, Khālid, 54
Murqus, Elias, 43

Nablus, 134
Nasser, Gamal Abdel, 5, 8–12, 19–21, 62, 66, 68, 95
National Covenant, 35–36, 108, 113, 114
Nuclear weapons, 44–45, 67

October 1973 War, 19, 20, 48, 100
Oil weapon, 46, 67
Oteifi, Gamal al-, 58
Ottoman period, 136

Palestine Liberation Organization (PLO), 16, 29–39, 49, 58, 76–77, 97, 98, 108, 113–115, 119, 120, 124, 125, 159, 160
Covenant, 35–36, 108, 113, 114
Eighth National Council, 118–119
"Political Program of the PLO," 37
"Ten-point program," 37–38
Twelfth National Council, 108, 114
Palestinian problem, 27, 28–39, 97–98, 106–109, 113–122, 165–166
"continuous strife" school and, 67
"dovish-dovish" school and, 130–131
"erosion and withering away" school, 44–46
fedayeen, 13–16, 17, 21, 76
"hawkish-hawkish" school and, 134–136
"reducing Israel to its natural dimensions" school and, 49–50, 73–76
Partition Resolution of November 1947, 10, 33, 35, 46
"Phases method" (Uslūb al-Marāhil), 45–46
Philistines, 135
PLO: *see* Palestine Liberation Organization (PLO)
"Political Program of the PLO, The," 37
Public opinion, 87–91

Index

Qabs, Al-, 51

Rabat Summit Conference
  (1974), 39, 56, 116
Rabat Resolution (1974), 39
"Reducing Israel to its natural
  dimensions" school, 19, 47–
  63, 66, 70–77, 123, 155
  schematic typology of, 74–75
Rejection Front, 76
Renan, Ernest, 141
Revisionist movement, 141

Sadat, Anwar el, 39, 49, 52, 55–
  56, 57, 73, 100–101, 103
Security Council Resolution 242,
  19, 28, 42, 54–57, 64, 108,
  111, 112
Security Council Resolution 338,
  56
"Separate treatment" strategy,
  21
Sharabi, Hisham, 57
Shukairy, Ahmad, 15
Sh'un Filastiniyya, 76
Siāsah, As-, 55
Siassa al Dawliya, Al-, 60
Sid-Ahmad, Muhammad, 57–60
Sinai interim agreement of Sep-
  tember 1975, 76, 104, 122,
  143, 159
Six-Day War, 10, 15, 17, 94–96
Sous, Ibrahim, 30, 33
"Strategy of Phases," 103
Suez Canal, 12
Syria, 10, 121, 125, 136

"continuous strife" school and,
  76, 77
"erosion and withering away"
  school and, 77
Lebanese intervention, 159, 166
"reducing Israel to its natural
  dimensions" school and, 77

Tali'a, At-, 58
Tel Aviv, 134
Thavra, Ath-, 51
Tiran, straits of, 12, 95
Trans-Jordan, 136
Twelfth Palestinian National
  Council of June 1974, 108,
  114

Union of Soviet Socialist Repub-
  lics, 69, 132, 137, 159
United States, 137, 139, 140

Vietnam, guerrilla warfare in,
  13, 14–15

"Weakness of the Fedayeen,
  The" (Harkabi), 14
West Bank, 14, 28–31, 37, 38,
  49, 97–98, 114–115, 117, 120,
  125, 131, 133–136, 166
Withdrawal question, 27–28, 42–
  43, 45, 48, 50, 64, 103–105,
  111–112, 125, 128, 133, 142,
  162

Zionism, 42, 60, 95, 134, 141,
  166

Temple Israel

Minneapolis, Minnesota

In Honor of the Bar Mitzvah of
JOSEPH WILLIAM PRASS
by his Parents,
Mr. & Mrs. David Prass

January 31, 1981